LOVE TO LEAD

Dr Tracy Kite

Love to Lead

First published in 2018 by

Panoma Press Ltd
48 St Vincent Drive, St Albans, Herts, AL1 5SJ, UK
info@panomapress.com
www.panomapress.com

Book layout by Neil Coe.

Printed on acid-free paper from managed forests.

ISBN 978-1-784521-46-2

Testimonials

Tracy has distilled over 30 years of her own front line management experience with recent and robust academic study to create a powerful and practical guide that will bring compassion and humanity back into the workplace. This book will benefit individuals, organisations and society.

Dr Val Lowman OBE, Founder, BeOnsite

A truly ground breaking book that reveals that love is the missing link that will take your leadership style from good to great and practical ways that you can put it into action.

Sophie Keller, best-selling author of the *How Happy is...* book series and co-founder of the Village Workspace

With the pace of change and complexities of running a business, leaders need to love what they do to do it well. Tracy has found an inspiring way to share her ideas to help leaders connect with and share the leadership love.

Dr Carole Edmond, CEO, The Regard Group

Acknowledgements

This book has been years in the writing, with a lifetime of research and preparation. I would like to thank my husband Mark and my family – Michael, Anna, Jay and Rowan – for the unswerving belief, support and inspiration to succeed.

Dr Val Lowman, Dr Carole Edmond, Katie Mansfield-Loynes, Paul Middleton, Sophie Keller and Helen Down – thank you for the challenge, insightful questions and critical friendship.

In memory of Dr Joanna Kozubska, my tutor, colleague, mentor and friend; and Jackie Field, always my inspiration.

Foreword

"There are two types of people – those who come into a room and say 'Well, here I am!' and those who come in and say 'Ah, there you are'." *(Frederick L. Collins, 1994)*

Leadership and 'getting it right' is currently experiencing yet another period of change, and this is accompanied by a plethora of books telling you how to lead effectively. Some of these books are skilfully written and presented whereas others merely re-deliver old frames of thinking. Every now and again a book comes along that you understand, provides practical help in identifying how you can improve and changes how you think about yourself, your role and the organisation around you. In case you're wondering – this is that book!

Having worked in the social care sector for most of my working life I recognise that it is hard – hard work, hard decisions, hard to maintain an effective work/life balance and hard, at times, to like yourself and others. I have lived through attempts at a 'coaching culture' which was seen as the panacea to an exhausted workforce that was forever changing. New buzz words were introduced that only went as far as explaining old behaviours. Then along came Tracy Kite, and the rest, as they say, is history.

I was under the impression, from the experiences I had endured, that coaching was 'touchy-feely' and overly therapeutic – not at all what I am comfortable with. With Tracy it became hard core, truly developmental and action/outcome focused. It was also not 'an added extra', it was about leadership encompassing coaching, and not 'leadership and I'll do some coaching'.

Tracy's work comes from years of research and practice. Tracy truly believes that leading with love, care and respect is the best way – and I have to agree. Facilitating your staff to become better at their role, truly listening to what is being said to you and adopting an action-based intervention approach – why wouldn't you?

Be the person you would want to lead you. Be the person that says 'Ah, there you are'.

Katie Mansfield-Loynes RN,
Cert Ed, BA PCE, M.Mgt (Dist)

Senior Lecturer

Contents

Introduction

As I walk through the leadership world, in whatever sector, I see managers who work hard, putting in lots of hours and ever more effort into meeting objectives, hitting targets and impacting the bottom line. They still say they love their job and that leadership matters to them, but success is measured through long hours, gruelling schedules and driving hard. But what if there was another way? What if you had the skills to tap into other resources, which achieve similar or better success results, in a much easier, more pleasant and human way? You get to love your work, achieve excellence without taking on more. This book really does offer that opportunity – the only thing you have to do is give a damn. About people. Your people. Those fellow human beings working alongside you.

You'll have no doubt read the title of this book and wondered why anyone might risk using the 'L' word if they're writing a credible and robustly researched text on leadership. Surely that's going to put people off – promote the view that this is just another lightweight book which might make you feel good but has no real place in the business world? How can love ever be any part of the demanding, harried world of the average manager, when after all, the priority is to just get the business done, to the highest standard? Why do you have to think about love (or giving a damn about people) when it's simple hard work that gets the job done?

Let me reassure you, this is not another self-help book. This is a leadership text designed to focus you on excellence – getting business done, improving the use of business resources and maximising the impact of your team. The difference is that it uses a human rather than a process context. It focuses on the fact that leaders are human beings too and recognises that in much leadership development work this is forgotten. In this text, leadership is about how each of us uses that humanity to its maximum, to drive business success.

So why mention love? I tried and failed to describe the humanness in leadership without it – it is a risk after all, when writing serious script. Given that you're reading this text, you probably love your work and want to keep growing as a leader. There's another context for love here though – a deeply human exploration of leadership that is people focused but continues to drive business. In Chapter One, I'll go into more detail about why it's so important to say the 'L' word out loud. As an introduction though, we could of course use several other words instead: caring, genuine, authentic, ethical, respectful, considerate.

You get the picture and I'm in no doubt that if I asked any leader, at whatever level of seniority, all would say that these attributes, plus many more, are crucial human elements of leadership. Sadly, they are attributes often missing in both leadership texts and leadership practice. Intellectually, we reel them off and acknowledge their importance without really giving it another thought. But what if giving it thought is really the key to excellence in leadership?

My belief is that this is exactly the case and this book is written from the stance that leadership is only effective when we force ourselves to face the discomfort of thinking about love. I mean love as a philosophical concept – an academic view rather than a romantic one. The one word that captures all the attributes we list above, plus many more, is love. It is shorthand for caring, genuine, authentic, ethical, respectful, considerate and all the others you can think of – it's about giving a damn. If we are to discuss leadership from the human view, we can't not talk about love – it doesn't make any sense, even if it is a word that went out of fashion long ago in business, and most managers who want to be seen as credible wouldn't use it **ever**. I'm arguing that it **must** be used to understand the bedrock of leadership and how we can do it better.

As further reassurance, you aren't going to be reading about love ad nauseum all the way through the book. There will a chapter discussing love in business, in depth from the outset. The rest of the work comes from solid business language, albeit focusing on the human condition. However, the foundation of business language, in this text, wholly rests on the philosophical argument that love is essential for good leadership – from the CEO down to the newest of leaders in the workforce.

This book is a practical guide for real leaders and managers in any sector or industry, at any level of an organisation, large or small; a guide which aims to help leaders, whether they are the CEO or a team leader new in post, to consider, reflect on and practise skills to truly get the best from their teams. The challenge, of course, is how to do this when those leaders and managers are already so busy; already inundated with work, wrestling with too many tasks in too little time or facing hundreds of emails, phone calls and demands in a day. What is the use of pushing you to do even more?

Doing more may promise an improvement in your team's functioning and capacity to do their job, but even with this promise, can you commit to any more additions to your workload? Love is an issue here too of course; as a philosophy, we might think first of how to focus that out to our teams, but in reality, it starts with ourselves. An inward focus of love – caring, genuine, authentic, ethical, respectful, considerate behaviour towards ourselves – is the beginning. I realise this sounds soft and unbusinesslike right now but bear with me. I'm going to convince you it makes hard business sense.

This book is written with that challenge in mind. It has been several years in the making and whilst it is written in an informal, easily 'digestible' manner, it is built on several years of doctoral research, considering the philosophies and works of many leadership and coaching thinkers and writers (as well as philosophers on love!). Most importantly it considers that you are busy! It assumes that you genuinely want the best for your team, your service and your business, but you can't take on lengthy periods of study or attend time-consuming training. You understand that business success is directly related to the performance of teams and individuals, but you can't make any more time in the day for leadership development, which requires heaps of thinking and study time. And you probably don't really want to think about loving your co-workers right now.

So, here's more reassurance: the knowledge, information and techniques you will find here are developed with an in-depth knowledge and decades of experience of real leadership in real organisations. I have been a leader and manager for three decades, at varying levels of seniority, leading large and small teams. Those teams have been employed locally in the same building and have been geographically dispersed throughout the country. I know what you are going through and I have been on the receiving end of those demands and expectations. I have also wrestled heavily with the concept of expressing love to my co-workers. But in that philosophical sense, I've concluded that it's impossible not to – even though there have been many times when I failed to do so.

The techniques described in this book can be highly effective in all leadership situations. They are built on the premise that the role of the leader is to get the best from the people they lead, ultimately ensuring that every team member works to their maximum potential and is sufficiently skilled, knowledgeable and motivated to achieve a successful and profitable service or business. Coupled with that premise though, is that busy leaders must contemplate and develop in a way that doesn't add to already impossible workloads. Reflection and development must ultimately occur, for leaders and their teams, in a way that can easily be incorporated into their busy schedules, whilst being effective and sustainable into the future. That development must be quickly effective and highly impactful for the busy leader to see its worth and invest some effort in practising and using simple methods to gain valuable results.

This book looks in detail at how leaders can make small changes to daily behaviours and adopt simple strategies and interventions to get the best from their teams. The focus is on creating optimum performance and enhancing services and outcomes – the core function of leaders and managers in the workplace. However, in doing this it focuses on being human. It sets aside complex models of performance and theories of business and management in favour of the human factor – the acknowledgement that people make or break businesses. If leaders can become skilled at managing wellbeing and leading others through healthy, meaningful and respectful interactions, even the most driven business settings can be enhanced and improved.

Coaching for Leadership

'Coaching for Leadership' is the phrase I use throughout the book to describe the techniques and practices of working with teams and taking care of wellbeing, using collaborative and facilitative styles of leadership. It is the language of love encapsulated in business form. In western leadership cultures, we can discuss the value of collaborative and facilitative leadership styles and there is much written in the literature about this topic. I'm not going to repeat or summarise it here, suffice to say that there are great authors on the topic and their work can be found easily in bookshops and online. That said, whilst we know intellectually that collaborating with others and enabling and empowering them to function capably is the right thing to do, this rarely plays out in practice.

At first glance, you will disagree with this; of course good leadership is about teamwork and partnerships, cooperation and group effort and we all want to think that this is what we achieve in the workplace. However, evidence would suggest, my own included, that this is far from what workers report from the behaviour of their managers. Interestingly, leaders report that they lead with coaching, facilitative styles and focus on the wellbeing of their teams and yet their direct reports say that those same leaders are directive and autocratic in the workplace – lacking in the attributes of love.

We'll explore this further in the Coaching for Leadership chapter, but it's worth considering how your direct reports would describe you as a leader. Would they consider you to be collaborative and empowering or directive and autocratic? Loving and caring or all about process? Giving a damn about them or only about the bottom line? This could make all the difference in maximising the potential of your team and you may be surprised at their answer!

This book will allow you to consider why collaborative and facilitative styles of leadership are so important to workplace wellbeing and to develop the particular skills of coaching as a leadership style. Fundamentally the guidance will take firmly into account the existing pressures and demands on you as a leader and will not involve enormous amounts of time or effort to make a difference to your leadership practice or impact positively on your team. Small shifts in the way we communicate and interact with the people we lead are enough to impact massively on capability, functioning, morale, motivation, wellbeing and much more.

The Neuroscience Evidence

Where useful and interesting, I have added facts and findings from the neuroscience research. Again, there is much interesting and useful literature freely available which lends weight to what we instinctively know about human functioning, including how we learn, change and interact with others. I have attempted to discuss this in relation to real situations in the workplace, to provide interesting insights into why Coaching for Leadership is a crucial set of skills for every leader. This is not a 'one size fits all' theory, simply a range of easy to learn skills and behaviours which can make so much difference to the everyday lives of leaders and their teams.

The Basis of the Material

The information you will read in this book is essentially a set of judgments and beliefs which I have gleaned from decades of working as a leader. I have seen how small shifts in thinking, skills and behaviours, based on the foundations of a little knowledge and reflection, can impact massively on the outputs of a team and crucially the success of an organisation or business. However, this is not enough – there are many thousands of leaders who also have the benefit of years of experience.

This book is therefore an amalgamation of two things: a written record of modules of training which I have developed and delivered to hundreds of leaders in organisations; and doctoral level research of how this training impacts on those leaders and organisations and the resulting return on investment. Through my research, countless leaders have corroborated the benefits to themselves and their teams. The resulting return on investment correlates to hundreds of thousands of pounds in savings on staff turnover; reduced time and resource spent investigating complaints and grievances; improved wellbeing and reduction in stress levels for leaders; and improved levels of responsibility and accountability in teams. We will discuss this further, later in the book.

You can of course attend my training modules to learn Coaching for Leadership skills and details of those can be found on my website information, located elsewhere in this book. You can also access my doctoral research, although the training modules and this book are both designed to translate the academic arguments into more easy to grasp concepts and guidance. My aim is that this book will enable those unable to attend training, or those who have differing learning styles, to easily access the valuable and effective techniques.

CHAPTER ONE

The Business of Love and Why We Can't Avoid It

I have been a leader within my job roles for almost 30 years at varying organisational levels. Even though my whole career has been spent in 'caring' professions, I really only considered the notion of love in business some four years ago, during my doctoral studies. Even then, it took me until now to recognise the importance of saying it out loud and writing it down. I had played around with the phrasing through all that time, and in my research I used a terminology of 'care' in business and more recently expressing the importance of wellbeing. I thought these words would be more palatable to the discerning business leader. Care and wellbeing are vital trains of thought in leading well in the workplace and I cover them in this chapter also. However, care and wellbeing are components of the overarching topic of the philosophical constructs of love.

I recall a surprising meeting with my supervising professor during the first year of my doctoral studies. She was a well-to-do lady with very many years of high-level experience in business and academia. She was somewhat forbidding in her manner, always challenging and insisting that her students were able to argue every thought and opinion at the highest academic level. One day I was wrestling with my thoughts around what it was that made my coaching work with professional leaders and managers successful and unique. I was floundering with concepts like compassion and care, when suddenly she reached into a cupboard and brought out a black drawstring bag. She delved into the bag and pulled out a life-size plastic brain and a large, red, sparkly plastic heart. She astonished me by saying, "Of course what you're really talking about is love!" which she went on to illustrate with her plastic brain and heart.

This highly focused, highly academic businesswoman was unafraid of the 'L' word and almost certainly recognised that I was – my subconscious hadn't even considered letting me say it out loud! I felt the need to be taken credibly and robustly in my professional and academic work and here she was giving me permission to consider why love as a concept is crucial in the hard, driven world called business. I will never forget that moment. It was so unexpected, it forced me into considering that what made my own work with leaders so powerful was an unconscious sense of love and caring – I truly did give a damn and I was able to show that in my working practices. That unconscious drive now needed to become conscious, so I could articulate it and share it with others who were also looking to be better leaders and managers.

Philosophers on Love

Love is one of the most highly contemplated and argued concepts amongst philosophers as far back as Plato and Aristotle. Philosophers have been debating it for centuries and continue to do so to the current day. Why do we find it so fascinating – and so frightening outside the confines of our personal relationships? That's a complex philosophical question itself; suffice to say it's probably so interesting because every human being experiences emotions of love to some degree. We can all relate to it and whilst for most of us we consider it only within the realms of our personal or spiritual life, we can all conjure up memories of how love makes us feel. It's a deep, complex emotion that appears endlessly in music, literature, art, friendships, romantic and spiritual relationships. What is rare, however, is for it to make an appearance at work or in business-focused literature. I do wonder why this is and there may be many reasons.

However, I think in the western world we have stopped seeing love as anything other than the romantic variety. If we reduce love to this category only, inevitably it has no place at work. I also think that we believe work has to be different; professional, credible careers have to be based on hard, measurable data, heavy workloads and tangible outcomes, all of which must be overtly calculable. We are required to behave 'professionally', which to most of us means to our status and position, without personal interruptions and distractions.

My belief is that in our attempts to be seen as businesslike and credible and to further our careers, we have 'over professionalised' our behaviours at work, to the detriment of the human factor. This may not be a problem if your only working relationships are with inanimate objects, but if you are required to interact with other human beings in the course of your work, this can only hinder collaboration and the facilitation of others to be the best version of themselves possible. This is why it is crucial to consider what love really means, in its broadest sense, so that we can become the best version of a leader we can possibly be.

At one end of the spectrum, love can be seen as a basic physical phenomenon – an animalistic urge which dictates our behaviour. At the other end, it is an intensely spiritual phenomenon, which at its highest point leads us to divinity. Take some time to consider what love means to you. Here I will focus on concepts of Platonic love (taken originally from Plato's philosophies), in this context meaning the concepts of love that are relevant and necessary in workplace leadership.

One might argue – as Aristotle did – that the first point of love is that we love ourselves. In a business context, this makes sense. If we don't have care, compassion and consideration for ourselves, we will never achieve the best version of ourselves as leaders as possible. Tired, stressed, burnt-out managers never make the best of themselves or their teams. This book therefore focuses on techniques and skills which leaders can use to create wellbeing in themselves as well as others. Aristotle argues that the ability to love oneself is 'noble and virtuous' – in other words, it allows us (as leaders) to reflect and act in a way which facilitates excellence, ensures consideration and equality, and enables growth and development in ourselves and others.

One might argue that love cannot be examined objectively, and therefore it has no place in business. However, we don't doubt there is such a thing as love, so ethically we should examine it – examination and contemplation doesn't mean that something shouldn't be considered conceptually. It also doesn't mean we will never be able to examine it at least partially objectively in the future; neuroscience now offers 'proof' of concepts such as learning that we were only ever able to consider conceptually before current technology became available.

Ethically, we need to consider the varieties of love which are appropriate – and of course beneficial in the workplace. Love forms the foundation of meaningful relationships and enables human beings to care what happens to themselves and the people around them. In our private lives, we are more likely to trust, be loyal to and maintain accountability towards those we have loving relationships with. Love forms the basis of mutually respectful relationships and represents a desire to see the best in, and create the best for, those we love.

If we can translate this love into the workplace, we can therefore also expect more trust, respect and meaningful relationships with accountability. We have to care about love and love to care (and lead) if we are ever going to achieve the best from ourselves and our people at work. Using a language of care can provide the structure to understand better how we can base our leadership on a foundation of love, in a way which is appropriate for business.

Care

This may at first glance seem an odd topic for the business environment too. However, it is worth consideration in creating that solid workplace foundation for leadership to be successful. My own background is in healthcare, so it isn't a huge departure for me to consider this within a business context. I appreciate it will be far more difficult for those working in industry, finance or other sectors that are determined by hard data and equally hard management styles. That said, I've never met any credible leader, in any sector, who says they don't care!

What is meant by 'care' in the workplace? At its core, much like the topic of love, the discussion about care is a philosophical one; philosophers have been working for centuries to pin down exactly what this means and it's surprisingly complex. We'll all have a different definition of what caring means, so as with love, it's worth taking some time to reflect on your own beliefs and definitions of it. Your definition and belief systems are likely to be dependent on your background, experiences and possibly even gender. In a 'dictionary' sense, care is depicted in two basic ways: as troublesome worries and woes, as in 'all the cares in the world' or as in the solicitous and genuine act of caring for another person, situation, issue or object. Either way, there are few models or descriptions of managing in business that mention a care aspect in either sense, although I suspect most leaders would intellectually recognise that both depictions of care are needed in the business setting.

So why don't we mention care in leadership and business? I seriously doubt there will be managers who say they don't care, yet we fail to discuss, describe or contemplate this aspect of humanness and interaction in our professional endeavours. I do wonder if in our attempts to become more professional we have lost these origins of leadership itself. Those 'soft' aspects of human interaction that describe the solicitous, compassionate attentiveness which facilitates change and development required to achieve the business outcomes desired – those aspects best described as love or care.

There used to be companies like this; Cadbury in the UK built its original philosophies on this concept and proponents of 'Servant Leadership' and still does. Is it perhaps an indication of the difficulty in articulating the esoteric nature of care, compassion and other terms that we have become afraid of using in the business arena, for fear of seeming 'soft' and unbusinesslike?

In the 'professionalisation' of our world and our enthusiasm to prove we are of value to our business, we have tended to reduce these aspects to a brief mention of rapport building and trust in working relationships. This is what we mostly see in the popular business literature in relation to this topic. In our eagerness to be considered 'businesslike' and 'value for money', we have focused our attention on outcomes for the business and producing a financial return on investment – proving our worth in the job role we are in.

These are all vital aspects of our work of course and I would be the first to labour the importance of being able to measure value, if our work is to be credible and appreciable to the organisations we support. However, the recognition of ourselves and others as 'whole' human beings – the sum total of the experiences, beliefs, learning, background and aspirations that make people the individuals they are – is also essential I would argue. It's essential in ensuring we get the best from everyone who works with us – valuing them, appreciating what they bring and caring generally, so people are enabled to come to work and do a great job. This will include all those messy, unbusinesslike feelings, emotions, troubles (cares?), habits and fears that we have become programmed to avoid in business because they are considered difficult, unprofessional or they aren't the concern of the workplace.

To do this we have to care and, by definition, we have to love. As leaders we have to both 'take care of' the business processes, objectives and outcomes as well as 'care for' the person. This includes at least an acknowledgement that the individuals we work with are whole people. The person they are out of work is not different from the person they are in work, even if the behaviours change between contexts. We have to care as much about what 'matters' to the individual as much as what 'matters' to the organisation. This is the only way they will arrive at work and remain there, working hard and achieving what they are supposed to – if they feel valued and respected. Caring is what it's all about; it doesn't have to be soft and unprofessional, simply a human interest in those we work with, to gain the best and ensure the success of our business.

Most of us are already experts – we have people and things we love and care about deeply outside of work. We hopefully also love and care about the work we do and the job we are in. Consider how you can apply that in the workplace and you will have a team who are further enabled to come to work and do their very best. This isn't the soft option; it's the option most likely to get the best possible performance from your team. Why? Because we come to work to feel valued, respected and able to contribute meaningfully to business life. If we feel this, we will stay longer, work harder and 'go the extra mile'. What leader doesn't want this from their team?

If leaders are able to reflect care through love, it is easier to challenge our teams about their performance and business outcomes. This is because they feel that they 'matter' as much as the business does; we all need to feel that what we contribute is important and who we are matters within the team. Care provides the safety needed to explore, analyse, reflect and challenge in order to make significant change. It provides the safety net needed to become fully involved in those activities which inherently carry significant personal risk (admitting that we might be wrong, need to change or adopt new skills) because the situation is safe, and someone loves us – that is, cares sufficiently about us to ensure the outcome will be positive and worthwhile.

Care and the creation of a safe place to work with challenge and difficulty is about acceptance and a recognition that individuals desire to do a good job. No one gets up in the morning wanting to be difficult or perform poorly! If the leader reflects a tolerance – 'cares for' their people – development can occur and outcomes can be achieved. Individuals and teams flourish and positive change can happen.

People are people wherever they work and great businesses are driven by employees with expertise, motivation, skills and leadership capability. Whilst achievement of business goals and outcomes are crucial, the development of the individual must surely be fundamental in impacting on the business. It is individuals who are the 'make or break' of the business, alongside the collective power of the organisational culture, which is also created by groups of individuals. If leaders can create cultures founded on concepts of love and caring, work life will inevitably be more comfortable, enjoyable and productive.

To explain this, I have developed a model of care for business. A model which describes this 'soft' concept in a way that reflects its value and crucial application. Through it, I hope you will come to realise that caring isn't an indulgent weakness in the workplace but a challenge for leaders, which if implemented well can measurably impact on the success of the business.

It incorporates three aspects of the organisation, which are fundamental to business success and growth:

- The business goals and expected outcomes

- The individual (the people who work for the business)

- The collective culture and behaviours those individuals work with and within

The concept of care (and implicitly, love) runs integrally through all three aspects. (See Fig. 1).

Caring For Individual Needs

Caring About Organisational Culture   **Business and Leadership**   **Taking Care of Business Goals**

Fig. 1 Model of Care in Leadership

Caring about organisational culture can be translated into the leadership skills and behaviours expressed by individual managers to help teams understand the ethos and expectations of the organisation. Any individual will impact on the context, culture and behaviours of the groups they belong to and, in turn, the context and culture will impact on them. People have to work within the confines of organisational culture – culture defines how things happen in the organisation and what will and won't be expected or tolerated.

Leaders create culture – they create the expectations and role model the behaviours which others will follow. To not care (or consider this) risks the creation of cultures that form from ignorance and unawareness. It also risks managers asking their teams to undertake tasks at odds with the culture of the organisation and so rendering those tasks impossible or uncomfortable to complete. You can choose to create a culture consciously, but you have to care about it, and invest in it, to do so.

The business outcomes and *taking care of* business goals, measurable performance and data are essential in convincing our employers of our value as managers. This area of the model describes the 'hard' information and the agreed performance measures that are required from established business processes and techniques. It is the area where leaders must challenge, ask the tough questions and facilitate clear and honest feedback. It is the area where a leader and their team must work together to evidence that effort has occurred for the benefit of the organisation. Again, to do this well and with awareness, you'll have to care about it. Caring comes most easily here as it's what is generally most valued in business. It is also what is most often discussed in the leadership literature and in popular media around leadership and management. However, it is almost never discussed from a perspective of love and care.

Caring for the individual and their personal development needs is the final point of the triangle and the most overlooked in the management literature in my opinion. It is also the area where the foundations of philosophical love fit most obviously. This solicitous and compassionate view of the individual as a whole entity, and the accepting and attentive stance of the manager, does not imply a lack of challenge, tough questions and clarity of feedback. In fact, this approach provides a safe place for our people within which we can lead: a highly challenging and demanding position where necessary. This is because the individual knows they are cared for with genuineness and authenticity by their manager and can therefore tolerate and work with the challenges.

It doesn't mean you have to be friends with people, but it does mean you have to respect your fellow co-workers and colleagues as equal human beings. This can be difficult if you're preoccupied with status and power rather than care and respect. It's worth remembering that status and power never create long-term sustainable loyalty and commitment. Without loyalty and commitment, you will never get the best from your team and you will never deliver the best possible outcomes.

Engaging as a human being will get more from your people and therefore more success for your business. This really is worth doing, even if it goes against everything you've been taught about managers needing distance and emotional detachment. Detachment is a good thing but only if it comes from a stance of genuine love and care.

If care is absent, we can easily see it. We see managers who disregard others, lack manners and behave in a superior way. In return we see teams who are derogatory about their managers and who work against them rather than with them. Anecdotally, most people I speak to are able to recount a story where they have felt less than conscientious attention, solicitous regard and respect or compassion from their line managers. This may be short term or transient in nature in the most part, although where it is more consistent in leaders and managers we instinctively know this impacts on staff turnover and retention rates, complaints, grievances and general personnel issues in the workplace. These are all areas which impact significantly on the hard metrics within the business.

What happens when 'hard business' is pursued, and love is absent? I would argue that all of the things we want to achieve at work – business success, profitability and growth – will also be absent or at least affected negatively.

Wellbeing

As with love and care, I have hesitated to use the term wellbeing because it can come over as slightly esoteric and 'soft' in fast-paced business environments, but the more I think about it, the more important it seems as a leadership concept. Richard Branson is often credited as saying that it is our staff that are most important, not our customers, because if we look after our people, they will look after the clients in turn. For me, this goes some way to an understanding of why leaders must look after the wellbeing of those they lead. Without wellbeing, our teams can't function to their best in the workplace – so when we discuss wellbeing, it is to create optimum performance. How can this not be of ultimate importance?

The reason it is so problematic to discuss is that we all have a slightly different view of what wellbeing is – again we can't study it objectively. Overall, wellbeing is the state of being comfortable, healthy or happy. It is difficult to argue that most human beings are more likely to function to their optimum capacity if comfortable, healthy and happy, but realistically these aren't concepts which regularly feature in business models and strategies. Intellectually leaders know these concepts are important, but they rarely translate into everyday leadership focus and behaviour.

Wellbeing links so closely with love and care that you can't really discuss one concept without the other. It's hard to imagine being motivated, comfortable, healthy and happy in the workplace without admitting that love and care form the core of these wellbeing principles. Governments are now willing to engage with the concepts of wellbeing and undertake 'happiness' surveys of their populations in an attempt to measure perceived quality of life. If I were a cynic I might conclude that it's a political disaster to have populations with low levels of health and happiness. The optimist in me suggests that at least somewhere, someone loves their fellow man enough to find out how they're doing.

We already know that happy people live longer. It's not a great stretch to also acknowledge that happy people might work harder, engage more, be more willing to take responsibility and accountability. Evidence certainly suggests that happy people are more productive. We also know that stress, depression and anxiety in the workplace increase ill health and therefore absence, which comes at huge cost to the bottom line. If you subscribe to this, you can't help but support the notion that leadership must incorporate love and care of our colleagues and ourselves. Wellbeing doesn't come from nowhere, it comes from a commitment to create environments which are conducive to wellbeing. You have to care if you're going to be the leader that creates wellbeing.

Of course, there's also the argument that wellbeing can be created without love and care – that it sits in the realms of stress management programmes and employee reward schemes. Indeed, many organisations feel they have this all sorted; they have high-profile stress management programmes and glossy offers of benefits for employees. I have worked in organisations like this myself. What I notice though, is that it doesn't guarantee wellbeing; turnover rates, sickness levels, complaints and grievances are still high. Why? Because leaders feel that this is enough and they don't have to bother to be kind, compassionate, loving, caring human beings. Throwing money at the issue just doesn't cut it. There really is no replacement for love and care.

The irony is that these things are free and so much more robust in ensuring business success through optimum performance. As human beings we are hard-wired to respond to others who show love and care through compassion and kindness. As I've already mentioned in this chapter, this isn't the soft option, it's the creation of work environments which can be highly challenging because they feel safe. To realise the full potential of ourselves and others and therefore create optimum business output, we can't not focus on love and care.

We do however need to know how to translate the philosophical concepts into real action. Understanding them isn't enough – we need to know what it looks like in practice and learn the skills necessary to achieve the leadership outcomes we desire. You don't ever have to utter the words love, care, wellbeing etc. if you choose not to, but you do need to develop the skills and knowledge to implement them in your work. The rest of this book is devoted to helping you translate love and care into everyday leadership behaviours to enhance the effectiveness of yourself and your teams.

CHAPTER TWO

Coaching for Leadership – A Practical Expression of Love and Wellbeing in Business

In the introduction, I mentioned that Coaching for Leadership is a phrase I use to describe certain behaviours, attitudes and assumptions. These aim to maximise the success of your business or service by ensuring the best possible performance from the people in your teams. The behaviours, attitudes and assumptions are developed on the foundations of the philosophical principles of love, care and wellbeing discussed in the previous chapter.

Coaching for Leadership really describes a simple set of techniques which focus on a leadership shift – the shift from a 'telling' (autocratic, distant, power-focused) style to an 'asking' (loving, caring, compassionate, human) style. This shift respects that there are many useful styles of leadership which are contextual and situational. Coaching for Leadership does not aim to disregard or supersede these; it is an attitude and approach to leadership which can be encompassed into many leadership situations and settings and which spotlight some of the skills which professional coaches use, on a bedrock of the principles of love and care. The key for leaders is to learn those skills and incorporate them into daily leadership practices and behaviours.

This book does not aim to create professional coaches; there are many books and courses designed to do this specifically. However, in order to become a leader who coaches – who displays an 'asking' rather than a 'telling' style – we need to look closely at the skills that professional coaches use, alongside love and care philosophies, which with practice can impact highly effectively on the success of teams and individuals.

Alongside those coaching skills, we will also look at skills and attributes often forgotten in professional workplace situations but which make an enormous difference to proficiency in business settings. These are abilities which are 'common sense' at first glance but which I believe have taken a back seat or, more worryingly, have become non-existent in the modern workplace. Interestingly, they are also attributes which sit within the realms of love and care: respect, trust and good manners. In our attempts to be professional and businesslike, we have 'over professionalised' the workplace and have forgotten that a foundation of good manners and care are vital in ensuring professional settings, where people can work together productively, positively, creatively and accountably. Where we have good manners and care, respect and trust follow.

Unfortunately, popular TV shows such as *The Apprentice* have led us to believe that ruthless, aggressive and back-stabbing behaviours are necessary to get business done or be respected as a business leader.

They are not! These behaviours simply make good watching and whilst they imply that manners, respect and care in the workplace are somehow soft and unbusinesslike, I would argue that they are fundamental business skills. As leaders we must work to incorporate them back into our professional repertoire. This does not imply laissez-faire or lax approaches – quite the reverse. It indicates that we assume staff will come to work, take responsibility for their job role and the quality of their outputs, behave professionally and care for their colleagues and the organisation.

We can assume this because as leaders we will be role modelling these essential behaviours, which will become the foundation on which we will make the shift from a 'telling' to 'asking' approach. The foundation on which we will ensure that our leadership behaviours switch on rather than switch off the thinking capacity of our people. The basis on which we will make the small changes that will ensure an exponential return on our efforts: improved quality of work, improved morale and accountability, reduced stress levels and improved wellbeing, reduction in complaints and grievances, and improved attrition. I don't want you to take my word for it, even if it is based on doctoral-level research. Life is an experiment, so get out there and have a go.

Good Manners

I often reflect that even in the most experienced leaders and managers, good manners can make the difference between an effective and ineffective leader. No matter how skilled or knowledgeable you are, if you can't engage with and build rapport with others, you will ultimately fail – no leader can deliver a service alone. Interestingly, you can find much in the literature on staff engagement and its importance in workplace effectiveness, but mannerly conduct doesn't get a mention anywhere. Perhaps it's considered old-fashioned or not relevant in business, but I would argue that it's crucial and worth a more detailed mention. It's most crucial because it's a simple way to convey love and care to those around you without saying the words out loud. Actions really do speak louder than words.

When we think about good manners what is it that we mean? This is worth thinking through for yourself personally. What behaviours specifically would you say are important for you and your team? I'm sure most of us would say that expressions of 'please' and 'thank you' sit at the top of the list of good manners. To say please and thank you appropriately seems to spell out the obvious, but I would hazard a guess that we have all experienced bosses who don't seem to think it's necessary to communicate in this way. However, I wonder what the consequence of not using please and thank you is to our teams?

The long-term effect of making demands and requests and instructing others in the workplace without such etiquette is damaging. It impairs relationships and damages respect between individuals. It causes resentments when one person believes they are too important or too senior to need to behave in a mannerly way. A team will mirror its leader; therefore, if you want respectful adult behaviours from your people, you must first exhibit them yourself. Saying please and thank you seems an easy way to start.

What else sits in the realms of good manners for you? Good communication with eye contact? Speaking calmly and respectfully at all times? Not interrupting when someone is speaking and allowing others to have their say? Using someone's name when you talk with them? Showing appreciation that team members are 'whole' individuals, including those aspects of themselves that sit apart from work? Behaving as if we are all equal and important in the workplace? Switching off your phone and offering attention when someone is speaking? Minimising disruptions during conversation? Finding out about and respecting cultural differences?

The list above is simply my initial thoughts; you will have many more and it's essential that you form some thoughts as to your own beliefs regarding good manners, so that you can consciously ensure you are mannerly in the workplace. Remember, your team will follow your lead. Sadly, I have encountered managers (I call them managers rather than leaders because a leader would never do this) who walk into a place of work and never make eye contact, let alone speak with those of a 'lesser rank'; who fail to acknowledge others' positions in the team; who speak over other people, or worse still, shout in the workplace; who believe their contribution is superior to others by nature of their title; who request time with their direct reports but don't silence their phone or minimise disruptions; who genuinely believe they are superior because they never shut up for long enough for anyone to debate with them or offer suggestions which might change their mind.

These are all examples of poor manners and they arrest the development and full functioning of any team, yet they are far more prolific in the workplace than we would like to admit. Behaviours like this push working relationships away from professional adult-to-adult connections towards parental, autocratic styles of leadership that switch off thinking capacity and create teams that are unable to problem solve or make decisions. They make it clear that there is no love, care, compassion or kindness in the organisation. Managers therefore see team members who come to work and fail to function as the adult they are. They use language which undermines their own position or push responsibility back to the manager. They disengage and fail to take accountability for their actions. They switch off and work at a level far below the capacity they exercise outside of the workplace – where love and care do exist.

What if leadership style could change this? A simple shift which begins with exercising good manners in the workplace. No complicated formulas or theories, or difficult to master techniques;

a shift which only has to start with the identification and role modelling of mannerly behaviour. It isn't difficult, although be prepared for some surprised reactions from your team. If behaviours haven't been encouraged based on good manners, this departure will be strange for people. However, that doesn't mean you shouldn't do it. Go ahead and experiment. What's the worst that could happen? Keep it up for a couple of weeks and see what changes. At the very least, you'll have a team of people who are polite to each other and the workplace will perhaps become a nicer place to be. I would anticipate though that it will be much more profound than this: people will begin to feel more valued and respected, which will provide you with a sound foundation on which to base your developing Coaching for Leadership skills.

Parental Leadership

When discussing love and caring it is sometimes easy to mistake care for something altogether different from the human, authentic, business-based care we have mentioned above. Unless we take care (no pun intended), love and caring will follow less of the business-facing model described and adopt a more parental, controlling style of caring. This of course will only serve to steer leadership styles back to directive and autocratic approaches, which switch off rather than switch on the capacity of our teams.

To illustrate this, I am going to borrow some language from Transactional Analysis – a theory of communication and therapeutic interposition. I am not going to spend time describing Transactional Analysis; Google or other search engines will assist you in finding out more if you wish. However, the language used is useful to describe this difficulty of caring in the workplace.

The theory goes that every adult human being has three potential modes or ways of behaving. All three are appropriate and contextual

– that is, we all choose how we behave, from the three modes, in any given situation. The modes are Parent, Adult and Child. In any situation, we will choose to behave as Parent, Adult or Child. There are no good/bad, right/wrong judgments here; all modes of behaviour are appropriate in the right situation and context, providing we read the situation and choose well.

Parental behaviours could be described as directing, teaching, advising and guiding, managing risk on behalf of others and nurturing. You will be able to identify many more parental-type behaviours and note that parenting is not limited to the behaviours of mothers and fathers towards their offspring. What is important is that parenting-type behaviours always assume that the other person is currently unable to know and understand as much about the world as the parent does. Therefore, the parent will be required to advise and teach, and ensure their 'offspring' remain safe in a world they know less about.

At first glance, parenting may seem an appropriate choice for leaders, especially if we are attempting to create a foundation of love and care. We can often assume that by nature of our management role, we know more about the work and organisation than our teams and we must therefore nurture them by advising, problem solving and directing life at work on their behalf. Interestingly, this is how many leaders see it and exactly how they behave at work. However, these leaders are most likely to be those who bear the heaviest workload; who find themselves reacting to numerous problems presented by their teams; who work long hours because their teams seem unable to fulfil their own roles without supervision and constant guidance; who never find themselves with enough time to concentrate on their own workloads because of frequent interruptions; and often find themselves 'on call' to their teams, even when they aren't supposed to be working.

If this describes you, could it be that you're parenting rather than leading? Many of us find this way of working fulfilling at the beginning of our management careers; it's good to feel wanted and sustaining to feel that your team need you. However, as time goes on you become tired and burnt out. If your team begin to function without you, it can feel like you aren't managing properly, but when they don't you become frustrated and wonder why they can't make simple decisions, carry out instructions or fulfil their job role without you constantly on their back.

If you are a parent of children, you will recognise all these concerns, but as a parent your children will grow up and begin living independent lives without you. Unfortunately for leaders who parent, their teams won't 'grow up' and the situation perpetuates until the manager is too burnt out to manage anymore. At first glance, parenting in the workplace doesn't seem such a bad thing, but as time goes on we can see that it doesn't get the best from teams and individuals or leaders. If people can't give of their best, your service will never be the best it could be.

Parenting styles disable other adults. On the surface they seem to stem from a loving philosophy, but really they originate from a controlling stance. You'll know this instinctively because you will see signs that the people who come into your workplace use language like, "I'm only a..." or "That's too complicated for me in my job role to work out..." or "You're the manager, you make the decision..." etc. Yet these are the same people who, outside of work, raise families, manage their personal budgets, make complex and demanding decisions, undertake altruistic and caring tasks, and don't leave the complexities and decision making to their own parents. So why don't they do it in work? Could it be that your leadership style is disabling those 'adult' brain actions and turning them into needy 'children' in the workplace?

Childlike Modes of Behaviour

We can all behave in a childlike way at times and this is perfectly normal and healthy, providing we are in the right context. Playing with our children, partners and friends is a natural way to behave in the appropriate situations. Childlike behaviours bring fun, laughter and creativity into our lives.

However, children are also needy, lack experiences and skills in life and may be unable to make appropriate decisions or interact maturely. The interesting thing to note here is that when people interact, if one is interacting in parent mode it will automatically 'push' childlike behaviours in the other. If you routinely adopt a parenting style of leadership, it will 'push' childlike behaviours unconsciously in your teams. And conversely, when they behave like children in the workplace, your parenting mode will also be unconsciously pushed. Ideally, you need all of your team to come to work and behave like adults (unless you are the kind of manager who constantly needs to be in control, with everyone else waiting for you to make all the decisions, and who is threatened when people are able to function independently!).

Adults in the workplace are those who come to work and undertake the role they are paid for, with maturity and awareness; with responsibility and accountability; able to make decisions and solve problems; able to self-regulate; and able to manage conflict and difficulty. Do your team regularly and consistently do this? If not, perhaps you need to consider whether you're parenting rather than leading in an adult way.

Adult Interactions

As I mentioned already, the ideal workplace conditions are where people come to work and do their job, with minimal need for you to watch over them, make the decisions and sort out the problems.

In the main, adults are able to do this for themselves, especially where the environment is safe for them to do so. And when people are enabled to work in an adult and independent fashion, the workplace is less stressful and people are more fulfilled. Your staff turnover rate will be lower and your complaints and grievances far fewer. You'll be able to get on with your job as a manager because your team are getting on with theirs.

A word of warning however: your team may well be suffering from a career lifetime of parental leadership styles and a lack of love and care at work, so will have become 'conditioned' to this. A more adult form of workplace expectation may be strange and confusing at first, so be patient. This is a journey, not a one-off process and you won't be able to turn your team into functional adults in the workplace in five minutes, especially if you're working with a long-term legacy of parental leadership styles. But it is worth persisting with so that you end up with a team of intelligent, intuitive, functional adults who can come to work, do their jobs well and free you up so that you can do yours too.

Hopefully by now I will have convinced you that there are ways to ensure your team work at their best, without you needing to undertake hours of arduous study or implement complex processes. At least I hope to have filled you with enough curiosity to carry on reading, because it's all very well to agree with and understand the points I have made so far, but quite another to know what to do about it. This book is a practical guide; I want you to understand principles of course (this is essential in convincing you that a small shift from 'telling' to 'asking' is so beneficial to you and your business), but you need to know what to do in practice. How do loving, caring, well-mannered, adult leaders behave? What does it actually look like applied to your daily work life?

I hope to answer these questions as we move forward on our Coaching for Leadership journey and influence how you do business from now on, so that you can achieve the very best from one of your biggest resources – your team.

CHAPTER THREE

Warming Up

There are some similarities to be drawn between coaching as a leadership style and coaching in a sporting sense, although I would urge caution as there are also many differences. However, one useful process borrowed from sport is that of the 'warm-up'. This section is a brief and simple opportunity to begin to limber up the brain to start considering the Coaching for Leadership topic and the skills you will learn. Complete the questionnaire below to begin the thinking process and consider your current knowledge of coaching in the workplace.

There are no tricks – remember, this is a warm-up. Equally there are no tricks or deliberate difficulties anywhere in this book; it is designed to aid you in achieving useful development with the minimum of struggle. It is also about committing to the principles of care and love. I also believe there is an analogy here for leadership itself – that is, leadership is about facilitating performance excellence in all of our people with the minimum of toil and complexity. Love and caring, whilst complex to contemplate philosophically, are hard-wired into all of us – we can all already do this! All we have to do is learn to translate what we know into appropriate skills and practices at work.

Tick the answer which you think is most correct: (answers and discussion come directly in the next section):

1. Which description is the most accurate definition of coaching?

    - A developmental process encouraging the potential of individuals and teams

    - The teaching of new skills

    - The provision of advice and guidance

    - An HR performance improvement process

2. Coaching is best carried out by someone more senior or more experienced:

    - True

    - False

3. Adults learn best when:

    - The teaching is formal – classroom/workshop-based

    - They are clearly instructed about what they should learn

    - They are given the space and encouragement to decide what learning is best for them

4. Which of the following is *not* an essential coaching skill?

   - Instructing
   - Listening
   - Questioning
   - Developing positive, respectful relationships

5. Which of the following statements is most correct?

   - Leadership and learning are separate things
   - Good learning facilitators and good leaders have the same skills and qualities
   - Leaders are born not made, so leadership cannot be taught
   - An essential skill of good leaders is that they consistently develop their teams and focus on learning and maximising potential

Your Warm-up Answers

It is worth noting that, as in all leadership areas, there are no black and white 'rights and wrongs'. Everything is open to a little debate and debating is itself an important leadership skill. We cannot and should not expect to always be right or have all the answers. Part of our responsibility as leaders is always to listen to the opinion of others and weigh this against our own. With this principle in mind, here are my own thoughts about our warm-up questions:

1. Which description is the most accurate definition of coaching?

   - *A developmental process encouraging the potential of individuals and teams*
   - The teaching of new skills

- The provision of advice and guidance
- An HR performance improvement process

This definition encompasses the nature of coaching as a leadership style, describing why we should be using coaching in the workplace. Remember that our definition of coaching here is always based on the philosophical notions of love and care. Indeed, for what it's worth, my opinion is that this definition describes leadership itself: of course leadership and management is about developing our people and helping them to be the best they possibly can be. If we achieve this, our business or service stands the best chance of being its most successful. It is an outward manifestation that you love and care for your colleagues' wellbeing without you having to say so specifically.

That said, leaders will always find themselves in situations where the other three duties described are also necessary. I am not suggesting that teaching new skills, providing advice and guidance or using HR performance processes are not essential leadership undertakings. Of course they are. However, if you are doing any of these, you will not be coaching, you will be doing something other than coaching.

2. Coaching is best carried out by someone more senior or more experienced:

- True
- *False*

This statement is false; it is entirely possible to coach another person or team without the same background, professional qualifications or experience. It is also possible to coach one's manager successfully, or those in more senior positions.

Coaching comes from a set of assumptions – that any adult already knows the answer to their problem or dilemma, or at least knows how to go about seeking that answer or solution, they just don't know it yet. The purpose of coaching is to facilitate another adult in the workplace to problem solve for themselves, in a way that suits their present context, situation and personal preferences. This flies in the face of traditional management, in that we mostly accept the presentation of a problem from our people and we hand back a solution, suggestion or piece of advice in return. We assume that our knowledge, experience and position qualify us to provide answers to others.

Legend has it that coaching behaviours stem from Socrates, the famous Stoic philosopher. He wagered a fellow philosopher that he could teach a street urchin geometry just by asking questions – and as the story goes, he did just that. He likely reflected genuine love and care of the street urchin through this approach – an assumption that despite his lifestyle, he was still an able and intuitive human being. Whether true or not, this tale provides the basis on which the assumptions of coaching are founded and the principles by which collaborative and facilitative leaders work.

3. Adults learn best when:

- The teaching is formal – classroom/workshop based
- They are clearly instructed about what they should learn
- *They are given the space and encouragement to decide what learning is best for them*

Instinctively we all know that when we are told to go to a training session, conference or workshop and it isn't something we are particularly interested in, we are unlikely to take much away in the form of learning. If we are motivated and enthusiastic because the learning is something that we have chosen, and we can see will benefit us, we are much more likely to come away with lasting learning.

That said, in sectors and industries which are highly regulated and subject to legislative training requirements, there may not be the luxury of individuals choosing what they will and won't learn. Leaders must appreciate that not everything can be a collaboration; there are non-negotiables in the workplace which leaders must be able to articulate clearly. They must also be able to explain knowledgably why the issues are non-negotiable – this ability reflects respect and compassion to others. However, these kinds of issues are much fewer than we might think, and where they do exist, there are opportunities to collaborate and coach others around the 'how'. I would suggest that if you spend your day telling others what they must do and also how they must do it, you are probably micro-managing them.

There is neuroscience evidence that would support this. Today we have the benefit of sophisticated technologies, such as fMRI scanners, which are able to 'view' the brain as it works. There is much recent literature available on neuroscience in bookshops and experts can now relate these learnings to many areas of business, including marketing, training and learning and of course, leadership and management. I will use some of those insights throughout this book.

The neuroscience evidence suggests that when one adult tells another adult what to do, it closes down large areas of neuronal functioning. In other words, sizeable portions of the brain stop firing and therefore thinking capacity becomes lessened. We know this instinctively – we've all had the frustration when we've told someone something several times but they still fail to do what we've instructed. Well, now you know why! In 'telling' them, you've switched off their thinking potential. This is a profound thought, so I'll say it again: when one adult tells another adult what to do, it shuts down the thinking capacity of parts of the other person's brain.

So, if you have a directive 'telling' style of leadership, you may well be working with teams who are functioning far below their actual potential. 'Switching off' people's brains isn't a sensible approach to developing teams and ensuring individuals work to their full potential. It is also not respectful or compassionate. You may feel that some of your team members choose to come to work and do the least possible; that you work alongside individuals who appear to avoid complex situations, difficult topics or decision making. But what if it's your leadership style literally switching them off rather than their lack of commitment?

Again, instinctively you know this could be true. The people in your teams routinely make decisions, become involved in complex activities and problem solving and tackle difficulties outside of work. So what is stopping them from doing this in the workplace? Could it be that 'telling' styles have switched off a full capacity for thinking, resulting in a workforce that habitually behave as if they can't?

Throughout this book we will be exploring techniques to switch those brains back on to their full capacity, so that our teams become thinking, intuitive, competent decision makers and problem solvers in the workplace, as they are outside of it. Can you imagine how amazing that might be?

4.   Which of the following is *not* an essential coaching skill?

- *Instructing*
- Listening
- Questioning
- Developing positive, respectful relationships

Listening, questioning and the ability to build a positive rapport with others are all essential coaching skills and come from a place of love and care. We will spend much more time on these aspects throughout the book. Suffice to say that instructing is not a coaching skill. This doesn't mean that instructing others isn't occasionally an important part of your role as leader or manager – of course it is. However, next time you find yourself instructing others, or telling them what they should be doing, think about how you might be switching off their thinking capacity!

5.   Which of the following statements is most correct?

- Leadership and learning are separate things

- Good learning facilitators and good leaders have the same skills and qualities

- Leaders are born not made, so leadership cannot be taught

- *An essential skill of good leaders is that they consistently develop their teams and focus on learning and maximising potential*

This is probably the trickiest of our warm-up questions as there is arguably a grain of truth in all of them – or at least something to debate. However, the 'most true' is our last suggestion; it is certainly an essential skill of leaders to develop their teams and focus on maximising potential. This is not a one-off task either; it's a consistent, ongoing description of the 'day job' of a leader, based on a solid foundation of love and care.

When your biggest resource is your people and the success of your business is dependent on their functioning and capability in the workplace, this aspect of manager behaviour is crucial. The remainder of this book will therefore focus on how leaders can achieve this, bearing in mind all of the myriad tasks, jobs, pressures and challenges you are already faced with daily. How exactly can you achieve team development and maximise the potential of all your people with a simple shift in leadership style, language and approach?

CHAPTER FOUR

Using Language and Techniques – Coaching, Mentoring and Counselling

In previous chapters I mentioned that coaching skills are essential to great leadership and to maximising the potential of your team. I also mentioned that whilst this book isn't about creating professional coaches, that great leadership is about incorporating coaching skills into your daily leadership behaviours, based on a solid foundation of love and care, this is what creates a collaborative and facilitative style rather than an autocratic and directive style. So what does this mean exactly? We have already explored the foundations of excellence in leadership as including good manners and caring behaviours, so how do we build a coaching approach on to that foundation? Remember, the skills of coaching used as a leadership style are the practical expression of love, care and the creation of wellbeing in acceptable workplace behaviours.

Firstly, we have to understand exactly what we're talking about. Coaching is often seen as an interchangeable activity between mentoring and counselling. However, there are subtle (and not so subtle) differences, so this chapter aims to tease out those variances and create a clear awareness of the techniques and skills you will use to make the shift in your leadership style from 'telling' to 'asking'. This is important as it's the coaching skills, as opposed to counselling and mentoring skills, that create the collaborative leadership styles, and which switch on thinking and functioning in individuals. This is why it's particularly important to create clear distinctions.

Again, there is much freely available literature around these topics and interestingly authors don't always agree on the similarities and contrasts between coaching, mentoring and counselling. What is important is that you use the techniques with awareness and deliberately, so that you can do it well. Therefore, I offer my contribution to the thinking and discuss my views of coaching, mentoring and counselling as separate (and useful) disciplines in leadership.

Before you read on, I suggest you reflect on and perhaps make some notes as to your perceptions of the similarities and differences between coaching, mentoring and counselling. Think about the role of professional coaches, counsellors and mentors and define what it is that these professionals do, what their intended outcomes are and the skills and techniques they employ to do it. As you contemplate the chapter, you'll be able to make comparisons between your thoughts and mine, to develop your understanding and create some clear language to describe these practices.

Coaching

There are probably as many definitions of coaching as there are coaches in the world, but they will all have the same basic principles. Coaching can be defined as a technique to develop others, help them to identify goals and achieve desired outcomes. It assumes that adults already know their own answers, or at least have the capacity to find answers, solutions and problem solve. The role of the coach is to aid development by facilitating others to seek and establish *their* answers and solutions. It aims to encourage thinking, reflection and seek creative ways of approaching challenges and problems. It is a way of provoking those 'lightbulb' moments – that is, to achieve a shift in thinking to achieve something which is sought after.

This shift in thinking is an essential component – because after all, if you always do what you've always done, you'll always get what you've always got. If you want something different, you'll have to do something different. A coach will help you do just that, but the difference, or solution, is that of the individual (coachee), not that of the coach. Therefore, the actions of a coach are 'neutral' – they don't seek to lead, direct or provide answers on behalf of the coachee. The coachee is trusted, as a thinking, intuitive, intelligent adult, to be able to reach their own conclusions and decide on their own actions.

This is more difficult to achieve than it sounds; in western culture we are raised to communicate in a 'telling' way. Most of our conversation is based around our beliefs that others must think the same things as we think. We spend much of our communication time in trying to convince others to think what we think, offering our opinions, views, experiences and advice. We do this for the right reasons of course and at first glance it appears to be a helpful thing to do.

However, we now know that when one adult tells another adult what to do, it 'switches off' the capacity for thinking in the brain. If we want people to think for themselves, be creative and develop fully, we must stop guiding, advising and offering our opinions. This is coaching. It is dependent on the love, care and compassion we have for another human being and the mannerly, respectful way we attempt to help them.

Coaching also requires a further discipline of listening well. We will explore this in detail later, but again, while this seems obvious, we rarely listen as well as we might. A coach will create privacy and quietness in order that thinking and reflection can be enhanced in the coachee. They will create space and safety for exploration, consideration and experimentation. They will encourage the coachee to explore their own thinking deeply, to question it and think differently. To do all of these things they must listen well – and to listen well they must minimise their own talking.

You cannot talk and listen at the same time. A coach will speak for only 20% of a coaching conversation and will encourage the coachee to do 80% of the talking. Compare this to a 'normal' conversation: it is likely that each contributor to a conversation will work hard to get their own point across and will endeavour to speak as much if not more than others. Next time you experience conversations at home or at work, observe how much time you and others spend talking and what components of the conversation are spent telling others what you think and feel about something. If you are going to coach, you will need to curb this instinct to share your views and instead encourage others to share theirs. Think about the most loving, caring people you know. I would hazard a guess that they are listeners more than talkers.

A coach will care more about the views, opinions and experiences of the coachee than their own (within the coaching conversation). They will feel it unimportant to share their own beliefs because this is not about them, it's about the coachee! They will facilitate the outcomes that are right for the coachee, not the ones that would be right for them. This can be difficult because when we are experienced and knowledgeable about something, we believe that our experience or knowledge is 'right' and we therefore know what the 'right way' to tackle the issue is. We feel justified in sharing this to help others. But what is help? Is help telling others what to do and how to do it? Or is it facilitating others to think about what is right for them and to find their own personal approach? A coach believes it is the latter, so what they themselves think is unimportant (for now) in the coachee's journey of development and problem solving.

A coach doesn't therefore need to be any kind of subject expert, they simply need to be expert at facilitating others from a neutral point, aided by curiosity. They must display excellent listening and an ability to probe and focus on reflection and changes in thinking. This is heartening for those leaders who are managing others who have a different professional and technical background from their own. To get the best from others and maximise their potential, we don't need to have all the skills and knowledge they do, we simply need to know how to coach: function from a place of love and care.

Focusing solely on the thinking and reflections of others is an altruistic act. It surely means you have to care about the person you are coaching and accept that their view of the world is right for them, regardless of what you might think. It involves a level of humility; whilst you know what would be right for you in a particular context, that doesn't mean it's automatically right for everyone else, including your coachee. This is why a coach spends time listening and facilitating the coachee to think for themselves rather than offering their own thoughts, opinions and solutions.

However, whilst at first glance this seems somewhat 'soft and fluffy', it most certainly isn't. Coaching in a leadership and business sense must focus on actions and outcomes. Coaching isn't a chat or a conversation. It is an action-focused intervention where the expectation is that something different will happen. In other words, the coachee will be expected to identify what action they will take, when they will take it and how they will feed back on the outcomes. The idea of coaching is to develop forward, doing something different and focusing on the future. However, it will only feel safe to do this when the leader, as coach, displays love, care and compassion first.

Mentoring

Mentoring is a skill used when we are endeavouring to facilitate learning in others. This would usually be when someone is new to a role or situation and doesn't yet know everything they need to know to undertake their duties competently and thoroughly. In mentoring, we are aiming to equip others with the right skills and expertise and the right standards and quality of work. We may also be ensuring they are able to work within organisational culture and fully understand expectations and requirements.

So what are the skills that a mentor needs and how are they different from those of a coach? If a mentor is going to ensure competence, knowledge and capability, they obviously and very demonstrably need to be an expert in the subject or context themselves. Otherwise they will be unable to identify what their mentee needs to know and how to judge that the required level of competence or knowledge has been reached. The appropriate level of skill and ability in a mentor is vital if new team members are to learn to function to a level of excellence rather than mediocrity.

By definition therefore, they will be passing their own skills and knowledge on to others. They will need to assess what the person already knows, what they still need to learn, how they might learn it and how they will judge that the appropriate skills and knowledge have been achieved to the required standard. To do this, they will need appropriate assessment, advising, guiding and teaching/ training skills.

We have therefore identified the main difference between coaching and mentoring. That is, a mentor's role is to guide and advise, whereas a coach's role is to facilitate and encourage others to problem solve for themselves. Mentoring is what we generally do most of in the workplace in our role as leader and manager; we have learned that the managerial role is to give others the benefit of our experience, expertise and general 'wisdom'. However, I would urge a large dose of caution: advising, guiding and teaching are all 'telling' styles of leadership. In a true mentoring role, they are of great value as a repertoire of skills, but in day to day leadership, 'telling' runs the risk of reducing the thinking, creativity and problem-solving capacity of the brain.

The challenge in leadership is to do less mentoring and more coaching if we want teams and individuals to function to full capacity, developing, growing and acting responsibly and accountably in the workplace. Of course, leaders must be able to do both coaching and mentoring, but the challenge is to coach first and then mentor when (and only when) the need arises. I see this as a continuum – a line along which leaders move on a moment by moment basis during the working day:

Coaching   **Mentoring**

The challenge is to remain at the coaching end for as long as possible, even when a mentoring intervention is self-evident. This way, the mentee is facilitated to use their own brain, thinking and reflecting to identify what outcomes they need and how they need to get them. Indeed, this is the only way to assess what an individual already knows. If we assume this and begin 'telling' from the outset, we set the scene for directive and autocratic styles of leadership. We also set the tone of 'switching off' the thinking capacity of the other person.

When we do need to move to the mentoring end of the continuum, this should be a conscious judgment because the individual is too new in the role or situation to know what they don't know. This must be based on assessment rather than assumption, otherwise the individual risks being disabled rather than enabled. Once the specific mentoring intervention is completed, leaders must consciously return to the coaching end of the continuum if collaborative and facilitative styles of leadership are to be maintained, and of course, if the brain of the other person is to remain 'switched on'.

Counselling

Counselling tends to be a catch-all phrase for therapeutic 'talking' interventions designed to support and progress individuals who are experiencing life difficulties or problems. Counsellors will be trained (as should coaches and mentors) and good practice suggests they will belong to a professional body and follow accepted guidelines for ethical procedures.

In leadership positions, we all find ourselves 'counselling' members of our team on occasion. What we mean by this is that we accept that they are human beings with emotions and fallibilities attached, and inevitably life's problems strike us all at some point. As leaders we will want to support our people through such difficulties as best we can, which is why we adopt some of the behaviours associated with counselling. Again, we return to the notion of care and caring for others at the centre of our desire to support.

Whilst I would endorse the need for support and understanding when personal difficulties arise that affect people – whether in work or outside – I would again urge a large dose of caution. It is incredibly easy, in our desire to help and support our colleagues, to get deeply involved in personal issues and difficulties that we are not qualified to deal with. Even if we have had training and development in counselling skills, it is rarely on the job description of leaders and managers to counsel others and this can be a very time-consuming activity. At best, we will consume much of our valuable time discussing deeply private and personal issues, and at worst, we may find ourselves out of our depth and deeply entrenched in something that we are not sufficiently skilled to deal with. This can have a disastrous impact on the workplace as well as the individual.

So what do we do? On the one hand, we acknowledge that we care, respect that our colleagues are whole people and that life strikes all of us badly from time to time. In these situations, we want to support people and ensure we take care of them, as far as our skills allow. On the other hand, we know that we aren't sufficiently skilled, it isn't on our job description and it can be downright dangerous to become entrenched in difficult personal problems. On this basis it would seem safer to assume that leaders should refrain from counselling their teams; we aren't trained to do it, it isn't on our job descriptions and we frankly can't commit the time it needs because of all of the other things that are on our job descriptions to achieve.

However, there are things that loving, caring, respectful leaders can and must do when life challenges others in our teams. Just because we shouldn't counsel doesn't mean we shouldn't support and assist where we can. We have to care because we value the person. So how do we value, care and support without counselling? We coach of course!

This is not to say that our colleague may not need counselling through their problems – it's just that we are not the best person to do that. Many companies provide counselling services or helplines as part of their employee packages. If this is the case in your workplace, ensure you are familiar with the set-up and know how to refer your team members to it. Don't worry if you don't have this benefit – most GPs or community walk-in services can refer people to the right mode of help for them. Don't be afraid to support people to access these.

As for your part, if you can coach, you can support your team members appropriately in the workplace, whatever the difficulty. Coaching is an action-based intervention, based in the present and looking towards the future. Taking action and doing something differently is a prerequisite, so by coaching others you are supporting them to explore, think differently and find their own solutions to current problems and difficulties. This is why mental health professionals are taking more coaching approaches to tackling even some profound mental health problems; it encourages personal accountability and responsibility and it seeks to move people towards a future which is better for them, determined by them.

When life strikes a member of your team and it inevitably impacts on their work in that moment, coaching will equip you to avoid caring from a parental stance and ensure you support from an action-oriented, adult position. You will be able to care for the individual without the risky descent into areas outside of your expertise and experience, whilst ensuring you don't load yourself up with time-consuming support, which sits outside of your remit. You will support with an eye on the future – that is, positively moving past this difficult time to a place where your colleague can re-engage with their work because they have identified the relevant actions and solutions which they must move forward with in order to achieve this. And they will do this because you coached them: you shifted from a 'telling' to an 'asking' style of leadership and you avoided advising them what you would do if you were in their position.

Broadly speaking, I would advocate that you avoid counselling in the workplace and leave it to those who are trained and employed to do this as their job role. They will always provide a better input in these situations than you can. Mentor where you need to; use your skills and expertise to role model exactly the skills, knowledge and qualities that you expect and value in each member of your team. Do this with awareness and insight so that you can do it well, but remember that if you do it all the time, you will inevitably 'switch off' the potential thinking capacity of the brains of the people you lead. Mentor only after a conscious assessment that the individual really doesn't know yet all that they need to know. Do this only when you are the best, most expert resource to fill the skills and knowledge gaps that you both identify and agree. For all of the rest of the time, coach.

Make your default leadership style one of asking rather than telling. This way, you can support, care for, respect and value people as fellow adults — and you can display that all-important concept of love without ever even having to mention it out loud. You can develop your team because you are neutral and can therefore allow others to come to their own solutions and conclusions. In this way, you will develop thinking, responsible, accountable adults who come to work, do their job to a standard of excellence and ensure you have the space to be an excellent leader and manager yourself.

CHAPTER FIVE

What Does Coaching Look Like?

In the previous chapters we have explored the basic principles of Coaching for Leadership and discussed the reasons why leaders may want to use coaching techniques, mentoring interventions and avoid counselling their team members. We have explored and understood the philosophical concept of love and why it is so important in leadership practice. We have debated why leadership requires a foundation of good manners, respect and care and how these essential skills can begin to assure that teams function with commitment, attainment and quality. After all, if your team looks good then you look good too!

We have also deliberated over the skills of professional coaches, concluding that leaders who wish to lead great teams with love and care would do well to adopt many of their skills and attributes. In a broad way, we have described this as a shift in leadership style from telling to asking. Not least of all, a shift away from telling ensures that our leadership manner doesn't switch off the potential thinking and problem-solving capacity of the brains of our fellow human beings.

To this end, we need to adopt skills and interventions which ensure brains are switched on, ready for action, ensuring that we manage others to function to a standard of excellence in the workplace. We need team members who can come to work ready to fulfil their job roles with the minimum of supervision and the maximum of focus, thinking and problem-solving ability. So, what are the skills that coaches use and how can leaders use them in business to ensure they develop their teams and realise the full potential of all the individuals in it?

I mentioned previously that this book isn't about creating professional coaches. Ironically though, the best way to begin to adopt coaching practices – those practical skills and attributes that ensure you approach all interactions from a bedrock of love and care – within your leadership style is to imagine for a short while that you **are** a professional coach. Once you have a clear vision of what coaching looks like, you can then incorporate some of the basic skills into your everyday leadership practice.

What Do Coaches Do?

Coaches create environments in which people can think, reflect, plan, review, problem solve and make decisions with creativity. They understand that in order to fulfil our potential, people need the space and safety to explore their own thinking and actions; learn to think creatively about what is and what might be; develop skills to tackle issues and problem solve; set appropriate and stretching objectives for themselves; challenge deeply rooted belief systems which inhibit learning and growth; and be supported to take action – preferably different actions from those they might take automatically or routinely through habit.

Of course, these are complex sets of skills which need to be studied and practised at length before coaches can unleash themselves on to the general public. However, they illustrate some of the essential ways that leaders can influence their teams to function competently in the workplace. We would all choose our teams to be efficient thinkers and problem solvers; to be able to set and achieve challenging goals and objectives; to be capable of growth and development; and to be able to act decisively and knowledgably within their role or remit. These are the attributes of individuals who are reliable, valuable members of high-performing teams.

Translating Coaching Skills into Leadership Practice

Picture in your mind's eye a typical coaching scene. The coach is there with their coachee and they are setting about working on a particular problem, goal or objective. Take a few moments to jot down what you would expect to see and hear. Before you read on, identify your own personal thoughts and perceptions of what might be taking place within this scene. Where are the coach and coachee sitting? How might the environment be contributing to the work being undertaken? Who says what and how? How much talking is the coach doing and how much the coachee? If you are a busy manager within a fast-paced work environment, the scene may seem alien to you at this stage. However, bear with it – there is much to be learned about skills that are transferable to your own context and in analysing how techniques from other professions relate positively to our own.

From our imagined scene, you might notice that the work is taking place in a private, undisturbed space. You might observe some silent moments where there is no talking at all – although you can see that much thinking is happening in those times. You might note that the coachee is doing most of the talking, with the coach's verbal input limited only to asking questions. You may spot that the coach has excellent listening skills; is able to reflect back and paraphrase what they have heard; is able to keep the conversation on track and focused towards the work at hand; is able to ask pertinent questions which help the coachee to think and reflect; is never leading, always remaining neutral and never offering advice or opinions.

You might also detect that there is an expectation of action. This is not a cosy chat, it is a business-focused, constructive dialogue from which the coachee is expected to take a defined action, to an agreed timescale, and to provide feedback and review of that action once undertaken.

So how is this relevant to you as a busy leader and manager? What if you could learn some basic skills from a coaching expert which would ensure that your team members were able to remain focused on goals and objectives, think and reflect on suitable outcomes and actions, and take specific actions in a timely way, feed back to you and review progress? If your team were doing this at work routinely, how would this impact on your service and outputs, on their role efficiency, and on your ability to get on and do your own job?

I'm going to assume that having a thoughtful, creative and productive team, able to work under their own steam with minimal supervision from you and able to problem solve efficiently, is a good thing. I'm also going to assume that the vast majority of leaders would appreciate having a team like this and understand that their service would be improved as a result. We'll now focus on the skills you need to achieve this – the skills that will take you from a telling (directive, parental and controlling) to an asking (loving, caring, empowering and respectful) style of leadership.

Creating the Right Environment

A professional coach will think very carefully about the environment where their coaching is to take place. At a basic level, coaching must always take place in a quiet space where there will be no disturbances. If thinking is occurring and this is frequently disrupted, the coachee will become distracted and unable to think deeply or with any consistency. They will also feel that the activity is unimportant and will therefore not invest in or commit to it well. The coach will therefore create a space where privacy is sacrosanct: the door will be closed, others will be asked not to come into the room and phones will be switched off.

Of course, as a busy manager, you will be wondering how this relates to your own environment. How can you possibly consider having time without the phone ringing or someone else wanting your attention while you're speaking with your people? However, this principle is vital if you are ever going to communicate well with your colleagues.

Creating a few minutes of undisturbed time for conversation with others doesn't have to be elaborate. Think about your own work environment: where do you normally have your work conversations with your team? How often do you get disturbed by other people or the phone? How could you avoid this? At a basic level, does the place you choose to have conversations with your people convey that you care about and respect them?

Think about places for communication that are away from phones. We're not referring to hours of conversation here, just those few minutes where you need to give that important information, feedback or support to a member of your team. Think about places you could go to be away from disturbances and don't rule out outside spaces; being away from the normal hustle and bustle might be just what the brain needs to switch on and become productive.

As well as being undisturbed, privacy is an essential aspect always considered by coaches. If you are having a conversation with a team member, make sure it is always private – it is for them and should remain with them. This is the case even if you want to congratulate them on a job well done or offer some positive feedback. It is certainly the case if the conversation is challenging or you need to offer some negative feedback. Humiliation or 'making an example' of people is never ever a mature, knowledgeable leadership style. We may create an illusion for ourselves of being powerful and in control if we can exert public disgrace to 'teach someone a lesson', but this really only serves to show how lacking in people skills the manager is. It creates resentful, disloyal and unproductive staff.

So, I'll repeat again, public shaming never works and always shows the manager up to be crude and poorly educated in leadership. Private conversations are crucial in ensuring positive working relationships and industrious teams. How can you ensure you create the right environment for privacy? You don't need elaborate spaces, just a place where you can't be overheard by others.

The creation of a conducive environment for work conversations also includes a level of physical comfort. People don't need sofas or daybeds, but a place to sit if the conversation is going to last longer than a few minutes is important. If our bodies feel uncomfortable, it is unlikely we are going to be able to turn our thoughts to being productive or creative. Don't rule out the standing conversation; sometimes standing to talk forces us to be succinct and alert, but it only works if the conversation doesn't carry on too long. Use a standing conversation when you want to be fast and efficient. Use a sitting conversation when you need longer, deeper thinking.

Physical barriers can also be a hindrance to productive dialogue. Try not to place physical items, such as desks or tables, in between yourself and the person you are talking to. This might create an air of defensiveness and reflect that you want to create a physical distance between yourself and your colleague. Even for the briefest of conversations, come out from behind your desk to extend a respectful, compassionate attitude towards your colleagues. Good coaches will never converse from behind a desk and neither do good leaders.

In summary, the right environment is essential to having creative, productive, adult conversations about work. A few minutes of private, undisturbed time which focuses on respectful interactions will create strong working relationships and will encourage your team to trust and respect you. Do the experiment – try creating the right environment for your conversations for a few days and notice what happens.

Listening

Have you ever wondered whether listening and hearing are the same thing? I would suggest they aren't, because for most of the time we only pay the briefest attention to what people are saying. We might hear the words that are said but do we really listen to their meaning? From a neurological perspective, listening takes place in the brain; we of course hear sounds through the mechanisms of our ears, but the understanding of those sounds comes from our brain. The processing of what we hear happens in the front of our brain, but not as efficiently as we might think. In fact, our brains on average focus only on the first five or six words that someone speaks to us and then we 'make up' the rest.

In other words, we start to make assumptions about what we think we are hearing rather than what we are actually hearing. Those assumptions are based on what we think the person is going to say, or what we might have said ourselves in a similar situation. These assumptions will be based on our own opinions, experiences and views of the world. We hear the words spoken by another person through the 'filter' of our own belief systems and experiences of the world.

If we're not careful, everything we hear is a product of our own thought processes rather than an actual representation of what people are trying to say. This might not seem such a problem in the first instance, but what if, day to day, you rush around acting on what you're being told by your team? Rather than your actions representing what the team are trying to get across to you, you're operating from what you think you've heard rather than what you've really heard. How much time might you be spending reacting to your own assumptions rather than being efficient with the reality of the situation?

My experience is that many managers waste a lot of time responding to issues and problems that were never the issue or problem in the first place. If we can learn to listen skilfully, we can minimise our brain's tendency to assumption and spend our time working on real situations. This is a good time management strategy – why would we choose to spend our valuable time on issues that aren't the real concerns? If you can get this right, you will free up precious time and become much more likely to spend your day making a real difference.

So how do we listen well? We've already gone some of the way there by considering the creation of a helpful environment for conversation to happen. If we create undisturbed, private spaces, we are already poised to focus better on what is being said. If we are undisturbed our brain is much more likely to be able to focus fully on the meaning being conveyed to us. Interruptions pull our thinking away from that meaning and encourage half-listening and assumptions.

At this point it is useful to put a name to good listening. In much of the literature, good listening is called Active Listening. I prefer Attentive Listening because it describes more specifically what is needed. To get a grasp of attentive listening, try another experiment. Next time you're in a public place, observe the conversations happening between some of the people around you. How do you know who is listening and who isn't? What are they doing differently? What do you observe about the people who are paying attention and listening well? Does it seem to make a difference to the conversation that's going on?

The most crucial aspect of attentive listening is to do what it says on the tin – pay attention! Attentiveness is a great skill, both for coaches and leaders. Many of us believe the fallacy that we can multitask, but this is a myth. Our brain cannot actually process more than one thing at a time; what it does do reasonably well is jump very quickly from one task to another, but this isn't nearly as efficient as paying proper attention to one task at a time. If we pay focused attention to one thing at a time, we will process its meaning and be able to deal with it very quickly. If we try to 'multitask', it can take up to 90 seconds for our brain to refocus on the task at hand each time we move from one task to another.

An example of this is when we're talking to someone and then we glance at an email that has pinged into our inbox. We may have been paying attention initially to what was being said, but in that brief moment when our attention is on the email, we stop listening attentively. This allows our brain to make assumptions about what the person is now saying rather than processing their actual meaning. Then, when we turn back to the conversation, it can take our brain up to 90 seconds to fully refocus on it, creating lots more opportunity to assume what is being said. This is an inefficient way of taking on and working with information because we run a constant risk of acting on unsound, partial information.

The crux of attentive listening is the full focus. The act of paying full attention to what is actually being said rather than what we assume is being said. When we pay full attention, we reap the benefits ourselves. The person we are listening to also reaps benefits: they have the rare opportunity to really be heard. This grows trust and loyalty in their relationship with you and they feel valued and properly understood. It is one of the most powerful ways you can convey the concept of philosophical love to someone at work, in an appropriate, work-focused act.

Attentive listening isn't a passive process – you will have observed this when you witnessed how people listen to one another in the previous experiment. Those who listened well (attentively) will have been showing this. They will have been leaning towards the person speaking; they will be making eye contact and nodding; they will have been making verbal indications of their listening – 'uhum', 'mmmhhmm' and the like. This is an active process which takes concentration – attention. It shows that we are taking the time to listen and understand properly, that we are attempting to really comprehend the meaning being conveyed and that we genuinely care about the person speaking.

For very busy managers, this way of listening might seem impossible, or at least counterintuitive. It is easy to believe that if we stopped everything to listen attentively to each person who needs to talk to us we won't have time to do everything we need to do in our working day. I am going to suggest to you that the opposite is true. If you take the time to listen attentively, you will ultimately save time. You will save time because you will be acting only on what is really being said, not on what your brain assumes is being said. You will not therefore be wasting time on things which didn't need to be done in the first place. Or you will save time on being efficient and only doing what really needs to be done by you because a little attentive listening means that your colleague is able to go off and take action themselves rather than you doing it for them.

So, here's the next experiment: make a commitment to only listening attentively for a few days. When someone speaks with you, create an environment where disturbances are minimised and you only focus on the conversation, nothing else. This means you have to put everything down and walk away from your phone and computer. Notice how the conversation goes – is it different from when you try to converse at the same time as carrying out other tasks? Is it more or less efficient? How do you feel about it and what is the reaction from the other person?

Remember that sometimes, by investing a little more time upfront (as in attentive listening), you create more time for yourself down the line as a result. If this works for you and your team, put some effort in to ensure you and your team reap the benefit of attentive listening.

Communication

I'm of the opinion that human beings are experts at communicating from the moment we leave the womb; newborns have a real skill at communicating their needs from their first seconds in the world. Unfortunately, as we grow up and enter the workplace we forget that we are experts and employ all kinds of unsophisticated communication techniques that end up bringing us all kinds of problems. It's almost as if we have forgotten how good we are at communicating with others – and sadly, when we are promoted to manager, some of us think that it's OK to stop trying. We forget that we are trying to work with people and start communicating as if we need to control them.

In the late 80s as a newly qualified staff nurse, an experienced mentor once said to me that the root of all problems in the workplace comes from poor communication. I've thought about this an awful lot over the past three decades and I still believe it to be true. When I sit and analyse the problems that routinely occur in the places we do business, they can always be tracked back to a communication glitch in the first instance. This therefore suggests that if we can get communication right, we stand a good chance of minimising many of the problems we spend our valuable time focusing on at work.

What does good communication look like? At risk of teaching my grandmother to suck eggs here, I want to take a moment to remind you – and it is a reminder because you already know how to do this well. All that's needed is for us to consciously remind ourselves that we already know how to do this and we are already experts – we've perhaps just forgotten how to do this well at work.

There's an adage that we should treat people as we want to be treated ourselves. At this point we might even say we need to love others as we love ourselves. This is true of communication and it's an excellent place to begin the analysis of what good communication looks like. Take some time to jot down how you prefer to be communicated with. Think of a time when you walked away from a conversation – not necessarily at work – feeling as if you'd been heard, understood and felt satisfied with the experience. What happened to make you feel that way? Where were you? Reflect on the tone, manner, inflections and balance of the conversation: what do you notice that made you feel included, equal and significant in the conversation? Why was this important to you?

Most of us would choose to be communicated with in a similar way. When I've researched how managers would choose to be communicated with, they normally say with respect, calmly, concisely, honestly, factually and with due regard that the conversation is happening between two (or more) adult human beings. For me, good communication always sits on a bedrock of good manners, which we discussed earlier. Respect flows from good manners and good manners flow from respect. This includes the notion that everyone has the right to an opinion and to voice that opinion – provided it is voiced with good manners.

Good communication has good manners and respect at its core and it most definitely does not flow from power-driven, ego-focused perspectives. Poor communication tends to be one-sided, manipulative or controlling rather than inclusive and collaborative and is delivered without good manners. Even very senior leaders identify that they want their line managers to communicate with them quietly, calmly, with a level of respect for reciprocal dialogue and discussion of differences of opinion. The poorest forms of communication are identified where managers raise their voice at others in the workplace and are derogatory or humiliating in their communication. The poorest managers are those who think shouting at others is acceptable in business.

We all know that the components of communication are words, tone and sound of the words, and non-verbal or body language aspects. Together these form the 'whole' of communication, but are you aware of how significant each aspect is in communicating well? There is much freely available literature about communicating, which generally agrees that the smallest component of communication is the actual words we speak. Does this surprise you? Some researchers think that the information conveyed by words alone during communication might even be as low as 7%! That is, only 7% of our total communication is words, with 93% of it falling into the tone and body language categories.

Even if it isn't quite as low as 7%, you'll know instinctively that words play only a small part in our communication. An example of this is when we can tell how our loved ones are: what mood they're in, how they feel etc. without them even having to say a word. Our brains instinctively process a whole host of information about their non-verbal, body language cues and we can read an awful lot of information from this. We are able to communicate quite well with people who don't share the same language as us, or with people who have lost the power of language altogether, because words play such a small role in our total communication. This isn't to say that words are unimportant, just that there is an awful lot more to consider when communicating well.

The issue of words is important when we consider how we are communicating in the workplace. In an age where business functions through technology, it is increasingly common for communication to happen electronically. We routinely send emails, texts or notes through social media to communicate our messages. In fact, I've worked with companies who almost solely communicate via email, even where people are working in the same office and could easily get up to go and speak with those they are emailing!

There is a huge danger in communicating this way because only 7% (or thereabouts) of our total communication is words. By emailing (or texting, social media etc.) we are losing a massive 93% of the possible information we could be imparting by speaking with people face-to-face. This is why there can be so much difficulty, misinformation and misinterpretation if we only communicate through the written word. Many of us have encountered difficulties when the recipient of our message has taken what we have said wrongly, ie interpreted it differently from how we intended. Therefore, we create problems that don't need to be there by not communicating face-to-face.

Many businesses are dispersed geographically, which poses a problem for face-to-face communication. If you are a manager who manages a geographically spread team, you won't of course be able to have communication in this ideal way all the time. However, you should seek to communicate this way whenever possible and use methods other than the written word to communicate routinely. Skype and other electronic video-conferencing methods are invaluable in ensuring we pick up verbal and non-verbal information when interacting with others, for example.

The literature suggests that around 15% of communication is the tone of voice, pitch, frequency, volume and speed that we speak. Over the phone, we therefore collect around 23% of the potential available information from communication. This isn't ideal but it's better than writing the message down – and unless you're a speed typist, generally much faster too. If time is an issue in your work, avoid the emails and talk instead; it'll not only gain you some time, it will probably also save time in backtracking on misunderstandings and misinterpretations.

If we are buying into these statistics, this leaves around 67% of communication as being non-verbal. This means that we instinctively take in vast amounts of information from body language. It is how we tell if communication is genuine and authentic (we can instinctively spot a lie or someone who is less than honest in their communication for example). We communicate emotions, intentions and desires unconsciously through our body language and it can rarely be faked.

Equally we develop trust in others from watching their body language – because this is how we interpret honesty in communication. If we only communicate through written words, it becomes very difficult to create trusting relationships in the workplace because the vehicle for developing trust is missing. In fact, in email-heavy cultures, it becomes a self-fulfilling prophecy where people feel that they must communicate in writing to 'cover their backs'. This is a warning sign that trust is missing from working relationships and colleagues feel the need to protect themselves from others around them.

Great coaches, alongside great leaders, have excellent communication skills. They understand that whilst we communicate in a variety of different ways, face-to-face communication brings the largest amount of information and therefore the fewest numbers of problems. Those who work with people based in different locations use technology appropriately, to maximise access to both verbal and non-verbal interaction. They understand that respect, equality and good manners are critical in ensuring successful relationships at work, which in turn maximises the potential for efficient working and enhanced achievement.

Silence

Silence is an effective and powerful tool in coaching interventions and it is a crucial element of learning to think and problem solve. Through just a short period of silence, the brain is able to think and process surprisingly quickly, which is why it is such a valuable instrument in developing how we reflect and learn. You may be wondering what place silence has in busy organisations and how leaders and teams might benefit from it? The key to great leadership is the skill of the individual leader to grow and develop their people. People who always work to the best of their ability and continually seek to improve are naturally those who achieve success and excellence. This is good for business. Therefore, any tool a leader can use to enhance the learning of their teams is advantageous.

What do we mean by silence? It simply means a little empty 'space', free of disturbances and distractions. No noise, no interruptions, no diversions to get in the way of what our brains do best: think! In our busy modern lives we have lost the art of using silence positively and we tend to fill our time with noise, entertainment and distraction. How often do you enter your office, workplace or home and just sit in silence? I'm sure many of us would say almost never.

There is a comparison that is often made between eastern and western cultures. In the west, we measure our productivity and busy-ness through how many hours we work, how full our desks and inboxes are and how many projects and problems we are working with at any given time. In the east, productivity and busyness is observed and respected through those moments in the day when someone is sedentary, with their eyes closed, desk empty and who is sitting in silence to think and reflect – meditate if you like. In the west we consider topics such as silence and meditation to be 'soft' and unbusinesslike. In the east, these practices are considered to be powerful and developmental – essential in growing the profitability of people and businesses.

To be reactive and largely unconsidered about our actions, may feel powerful and important in business; the right thing to do to reflect our prominence and worth to our teams and the organisation. However, there is much to be learned from the power of silence and reflection. Quieting our brain to allow for deep thinking and reflection enhances our judgments, problem solving and planning abilities. Through silence we can augment our leadership skills and make more considered judgments and decisions. This is an act of self-love. We can also use and encourage silence in our conversations with colleagues to support them to do the same.

The problem is that we aren't used to silence – it seems very strange when it occurs. We find ourselves feeling awkward and uncomfortable and we become anxious to fill the silence in order to relieve this. If silence occurs during conversation, we feel obligated to fill it. If silence occurs when we are on our own, we tend to relieve the unease by playing music, switching on the TV or distracting ourselves with social media. Filling the silence means that we are missing out on the power of deep thinking and reflection, so whilst it might feel somewhat alien in the beginning, practising working with silence is an essential leadership skill.

Here's the next experiment. Start by creating some comfort with silence on your own: spend a few minutes (this is all you need unless you want to take more) each day creating some silent time. Clear the environment around you and turn off all the noise and visual stimulation. Find something peaceful to look at or close your eyes. Notice how you feel – don't try to do anything with it, just observe it. In the beginning you will feel like you're just tolerating it. As time goes on and you practise more, you'll notice your thinking. You'll notice that it gets easier and that the time passes quicker. You'll relax and be able to consider things more deeply and calmly.

Once you're feeling pretty comfortable with silence in your own company, you'll feel more confident to create it within conversations. Of course, you'll have to be patient with others – they probably won't be as confident as you and will initially try to fill the silence too. However, you could invite them to take a few moments to think things through quietly and you can role model by remaining silent yourself. Note whether your conversations become more productive over time. Notice whether your thinking, judgments and problem solving become more productive over time too.

Questions

The ability to ask relevant, insightful questions is probably the most essential of all coaching skills. Because it is such a crucial skill, I have devoted a whole chapter to the topic later on. This section prepares for that by way of introduction.

Questions are an essential component of adult, evenly-balanced communication and form the core of all coaching interventions. Because coaching is all about the coachee rather than the coach, most of the discourse from the coach will be in the form of questions. The coach's aim is to provoke creative thinking and to grow and develop the coachee, which takes place through the asking of appropriate and challenging questions.

Questioning is also a useful way of encouraging silence. If a perceptive, taxing question is posed, the brain is much more likely to consider it deeply if silence is encouraged; distractions get in the way of our ability to consider profoundly our thoughts and answers to questions. If we are posing a question, we want the person to consider it fully and intensely before they answer.

The ability to question well is a skill which must be learned and practised. In western culture, particularly in business, most of our conversation is designed to persuade others to listen to our opinions and think the same things that we think. Therefore, the ability to ask questions is an intense shift in the core reason for conversing with others – it is the shift from telling to asking. You can't make a shift from telling to asking without moving from controlling the conversation to questioning.

The first skill in asking a great question is to stop thinking that you have to tell people things – you don't. You have to remind yourself that you are speaking with another adult who, under the right conditions, is fully able to seek solutions to problems, work things out and to learn and develop under their own steam. If you carry on telling them – giving them the 'benefit' of your knowledge and experience – you will inhibit those processes and disable productive thinking. Unless you need robots in your workplace, this is never a good thing.

The second skill in asking a great question is the ability to stop talking yourself. Good coaches and great leaders know when to shut up. They have the insight to understand that the best work is not being done all the while they are talking, it is done when they ask insightful and relevant questions, facilitate the conditions for others to consider and reflect on those questions and then support them to articulate their answers. It requires excellent attentive listening skills – even the most superior question is wasted if you don't take the time to listen to and explore the answer!

We all know managers who love the sound of their own voice; they sit in meetings and dominate the conversation, completely oblivious to the frustrations of those around them. Incessant babbling inhibits thinking, reflection and productivity. I believe that the ability to remain quiet and interject only to ask an 'elegant' question, listening attentively to the answer and considering this thoughtfully, is a measure of a mature, highly skilled leader. It is also a great measure of the ability to reflect a loving, caring and respectful stance appropriately at work. Where such leadership skills are cultivated, highly able, creative and productive teams are formed.

The ability to ask questions grows with experience and practice – much practice! In order to ask great questions, the questioner must first come from a place of curiosity – an inbuilt interest in the person, what the person has to say and in the conversation itself. My experience is that when a person tells you something, the first pieces of information they give you are generally not the crux of the issue. They are usually symptoms of, or peripheral issues around, the subject matter. If you just accept at face value what someone is saying, fail to ask questions or be curious about it, then spend time trying to persuade them to think what you think, life becomes all about the narrow thoughts of one person. At best we constantly shut down potentially creative and satisfying conversations, and at worst we disable others from thinking and acting with their brains in the 'on' position.

So great questions come from interest – also an act of love; an intense curiosity to know as much as possible about what the person is trying to tell you. You can help them uncover the specifics and detail of exactly what they are trying to say, in order that you can move forward with clarity. It might feel that this is too time-consuming and you are too busy to converse with your team in this way, but you will save time later on because you will be discussing the real issues, not the interpreted ones. You will also have colleagues who feel valued because you are interested enough to ask questions, and who have fully functioning thinking and reflective capacity because your questions have switched their brains into the 'on' position.

Great questions come from a place of inquisitiveness, through leaders who know when to be quiet. Leaders who use questions over 'telling' have a sophisticated understanding of how brains think and how inhibiting it is for one person to dominate conversation. They use questions to encourage silent reflection and attentive listening to encourage creative productivity in the workplace and to ensure the development of their people. Next time you want to speak in a conversation, ask a question instead of making a statement or sharing an opinion. Notice what happens and observe the potential to change the direction of the dialogue. How does it leave you and your partner in conversation feeling?

CHAPTER SIX

What Else Do Coaches Do?

'Holding' the Coaching Conversation

In his book *On Dialogue* the author David Bohm discusses the nature of verbal interactions between people. He has researched the characteristics of verbal exchanges between people and through cultures. He reflects on the westernised penchant for the domination of conversation and the inclination we have to readily interject with our own thoughts, opinions and experiences. He has observed how inhibiting this is to free, honest conversation and compares this style to an ethnographic study of small American Indian tribes.

Within the tribe he studied, the group would come together regularly to speak with one another. During these gatherings, each individual was at liberty to speak freely about any issue or topic important to them in that moment. The rest of the group were silent – listening attentively, only interrupting to ask questions for clarification. Everyone had the opportunity to speak of their own issues, in turn.

What was remarkable was that no one attempted to redirect, disagree with, contradict or offer their own opinions about anything said by someone else. The conversation was simply 'held' by the group – no one tried to do anything with it. They were silently supportive of the speaker through attentive listening. Once everyone had had their opportunity to talk, the group dispersed and went about their daily business as usual.

Bohm began to realise that this method of verbal interaction enabled this group of people to work harmoniously together, making decisions for the good of the whole group without needing to seek additional checks or authority. This seemed to be because there was a profound, mutual understanding of the significant issues in the lives of each group member, which was accepted rather than engineered by the wider group.

I am always deeply moved by this story; we make work life so complex when, as managers, we are hell-bent on making sure that our teams think and speak in the same way that we do. We feel that unless everyone is 'singing from the same hymn sheet' we are not doing our jobs well and our teams are not successful. Of course, teams need to pull together with a shared vision and committed objectives, but what if we looked at achieving this in a different, simpler way?

What is extraordinary about Bohm's observation of dialogue is that there was a much stronger appreciation of 'team', joint working and shared objectives when the conversation was simply 'held' by the group. Without the attempts of everyone else to sway the conversation or shift it towards their own life and experiences, there was mutual respect and understanding of the needs of everyone. Individuals were empowered to go about their lives, making decisions for the greater good of the whole tribe because they fully understood every individual's priorities in that moment. It seems that objectives are met and roles are fulfilled much more successfully (and simply) when we stop thinking that everyone else must think the same things as us, and realise it is OK for us all to have different thoughts and priorities. The key is the respect of others' thoughts and the ability to 'hold' those – accept them, as opposed to attempting to merge them with our own.

I can't help but wonder what the workplace would look like if we could achieve this. Coaches will hold and support the dialogue without influencing it, keeping the coachee focused on their own agenda, which encourages the flow of thinking and processing by that person. Thinking and processing leads to creativity, clarity, accountability and problem solving. It isn't a stretch to see how valuable this is for leaders to encourage – for themselves and their teams.

It strikes me that staff meetings for example could look very different. We all know the feeling of dragging ourselves along to meetings where one person dominates the proceedings and we sit and listen to copious amounts of information. What would it be like if everyone had an equal time to speak, to share their thoughts about the issues and priorities, without fear of judgment or attempts to get them to change their mind? To know that whilst not everyone's ideas or thinking can always be utilised, people are respected for their contributions anyway?

It is unrealistic to think that we can change working culture overnight, but there is an experiment to be done here. Next time someone has a conversation with you, try to keep it about them rather than you. You can do this by attentively listening and asking questions rather than offering advice and opinion. If they say something that is at odds with your own thoughts, try to just hold the dialogue – you don't have to persuade them to think as you do. It's OK to be different – new ideas and innovation come from this.

At your next meeting, shift the focus of your agenda. Rather than going armed with a list of things to tell your team about, try a list of questions instead. Make it clear that everyone is welcome to say what they think. Hold the conversations rather than attempting to direct them and listen attentively to what is being said. Rather than attempting to achieve consensus, respect and consider the diversity of thoughts put forward. Allow this to shape your decision making moving forward.

It is likely that the first few times you try this you'll feel less than successful. Not only does it go against much of what you find natural about communicating and working, it will also be alien to your team around you. But persevere – after the first few times people will relax and begin to communicate in a different way. Providing the conversation is held with genuineness, people will speak more freely, and your group time will become more honest, innovative and productive. Who knows how your team might flourish?

Privacy and Confidentiality

One thing that we would accept as a given if engaging a professional coach would be that our sessions would be private and would remain confidential. It is unlikely that we would participate if we weren't assured of this – not because we plan to discuss deep, dark aspects of ourselves, just because most of us work more freely and honestly if we are secure that we won't be overheard or have our information shared publicly. A coach will take their responsibility for privacy and confidentiality very seriously – their professional reputation will depend on it. But how many managers take their responsibility for these things seriously? Do leaders believe this is important and if so, why?

Throughout my research, most leaders have said that being approachable is important to them. They value the fact that their staff feel comfortable to talk to them about important issues and want to maintain this manner of working with their teams. Without a fundamental regard for privacy and confidentiality, leaders cannot hope to be considered sufficiently trustworthy to be approachable by their teams. A lack of privacy and confidentiality can seriously impact on the quality of relationships in the workplace.

Privacy describes the environment which the leader creates to ensure that information or the content of a conversation is not overheard or accidently shared with others. Whilst we all understand the concept of privacy, many managers disregard its importance in the workplace. We feel justified in having conversations or giving feedback in public workspaces because we haven't interpreted that there is anything that can't be revealed to others. However, people feel protective over all kinds of information and are much more likely to speak freely and honestly if offered the courtesy of some privacy. Creating appropriately private conditions for dialogue to occur is essential if trust and honesty are to prevail. It's a simple consideration which may make the world of difference to how your team feel valued by you.

Confidentiality describes what is done with information – verbal or written – following a conversation or meeting. Without confidentiality, privacy is pointless. People need to know that their information is safe with you and that you will not share it without their permission. Again, as leaders we may perceive that information imparted to us isn't particularly sensitive, but we cannot know what is sensitive to others and what isn't. Good manners dictate that we regard all information as sensitive if it isn't about ourselves.

Of course, we are all free to disclose our own information as we choose. But being a leader doesn't give us permission to own and use information about others at will.

There are times when we cannot keep information to ourselves, but the golden rule is that anything should only be shared on a 'need to know' basis. Honesty and transparency about shared information is essential in maintaining trusting, strong working relationships. If you need to share, let your people know this is the case and help them to understand why. Above all, if you create a culture where privacy and confidentiality are a given unless otherwise stated, you create teams who feel valued and respected and who are more likely to develop constructive working relationships with you.

Empathy, Trust and Rapport

We have already explored a little about the area of trust and trusting relationships at work. Professional coaches rely on trust to do their work – that their coachee trusts them to do good work together; that their information will be kept confidential; that their practices are ethical and professional etc. These are the foundations on which the coaching work depends, and productive work won't take place without them.

Arguably, this is the same of leaders and managers. We all appreciate that we have more confidence, take more responsibility and have more faith in our leaders if we can rely on our strong, trusting relationship with them. However, if the relationship is poor – we have no faith in their abilities and professionalism, they aren't confidential with our information or they don't communicate with respect and good manners for example – we are much more likely to abdicate responsibility, lack confidence or even sabotage their work. It therefore makes sense for leaders to consider and work on building strong, trusting relationships with their people.

This does not mean friendship – although inevitably we will be drawn more to some people than others. This is just the chemistry of life! However, whether we would choose to become friends with someone or not, it is still possible to form healthy, professional relationships with everyone we work with because each of these principles sits firmly on the foundation of love. Just reflect for a moment on the components of a good relationship – not a friendship necessarily, but the relationships you have with people in your life which you would judge as successful and satisfying. Jot down what makes it so.

We all judge things slightly differently in life, but there are fundamentals without which there can never be great working relationships. We have already discussed love at length and the aspects of respect, care and good manners; we have also reflected on great communication, confidentiality and the ability to hold a conversation without engineering it to our own ways of thinking. You don't have to be friends to do this; leaders can offer these skills to everyone and it is known as building rapport. There is much in the literature discussing the need for building rapport – both in leadership and in coaching – but few break it down so that we can understand exactly how to do it.

Rapport also doesn't happen without trust, and conversely trust doesn't happen without rapport. Both go hand in hand and are dependent on one another. They are both very easy to destroy; one small lapse in confidentiality, one disrespectful comment or one conversation where a leader only half-listens to an important message, could be all it takes to damage a relationship. The change from a telling style of leadership to an asking style – the adoption of a coaching approach to leadership – is a lifestyle choice. One which involves a 'human' approach to our role and our teams which, by definition, must include an attitude of respect, good manners, skilled communication and a sense of care about our work and people.

The concept of empathy is also core to strong relationships and is linked to our previous discussions regarding love, care and respect. Many of us have an intuitive sense of the need for empathy, but it is a difficult topic to pin down and understand. We may also confuse empathy with sympathy, but there is a world of difference between the two and it is essential to understand why sympathy is unhelpful in the workplace and why empathy is essential.

Sympathy is the act of commiserating with or pitying the plight of another. When sympathising we plunge ourselves into the emotional predicament of the other person and engage personally with their feelings, perhaps even sharing those feelings in that moment. We offer platitudes and comforting words, colluding with their situation. We all need sympathy at times in our lives, to know that those we care about also care enough about us to immerse themselves in our emotions and difficulties when we need it. However, this is the realm of personal friendship and family and is not helpful at work.

The reason it isn't helpful at work is that work requires us to remain focused in our support of others. We can be loving and compassionate without needing to engage with the same emotions; identifying too closely with the emotions of others is personally draining and inhibits rational, productive thinking. At work, leaders need to remain balanced and reasonable; still respectfully supportive but judicious and purposeful rather than immersed in emotion. The way to achieve this is through empathy.

Empathy requires us to understand others implicitly – that is, to comprehend that all human beings are different. Every adult human being is a product of their background, upbringing, experiences and learning. Because no one ever goes through life in exactly the same way, every individual develops their own unique way of looking at the world: their own sets of beliefs, attitudes, values and their own ways of coping and behaving as a result. No one does this in exactly the same way as anyone else. Therefore, you may experience a particular event in life and behave in a certain way as a result.

Another person may encounter exactly the same event but will react, think and cope with it differently because you are both different people with different life experiences to date. There are no rights and wrongs here, this is just the way of the world. But to have empathy, you must first understand this and then allow your understanding to direct how you respond to others.

Empathy is often described as 'walking a mile in another man's shoes', but this isn't the true nature of empathy. If you can imagine how you might feel if you were experiencing the predicament of another individual, you are halfway there, but it is more complex than this. True empathy is the ability to imagine what it must be like for that person, with their unique upbringing, experiences, beliefs, etc., to be experiencing their predicament. This is something very different from how you would look at it. It is of course impossible to do in a true sense; you will never be that person, so how would you know how they are thinking and feeling about it in that moment? You couldn't possibly, but if you have a strong rapport with them, if you've actively listened to what they have to say, and you have 'held' their conversation without manipulating it towards your own experiences and preferences, you will be doing a good job of empathising.

From this perspective you can remain supportive, but focused and productive in a way which doesn't emotionally drain you. Slightly emotionally removed is the best place to be – not unloving, uncaring or lacking compassion but concerned and attentive in a way that allows you to think rationally and offer appropriate support. If you are not immersed in the emotion yourself, you are free to listen attentively, ask questions from a place of interest and genuine concern and to identify rationally how you can help, from an adult, professional stance.

Pinning It Down

Coaching is an action-oriented, focused approach to thinking, developing and changing. From an outside view, some may think it is just a conversation – a place for someone to come and offload and chat to an interested party. This could not be further from the truth. Leadership coaching is business focused and carries an expectation that the coachee will take action, feed back on that action and analyse the outcome of the action to encourage further learning. In order to achieve this, a professional coach will negotiate and confirm expectations of action – that is, they will take time to 'pin down' with the coachee exactly what action they commit to taking, when that action will take place and how they will report back on the outcomes.

This technique is a valuable leadership tool, particularly if we often find ourselves wondering why people don't always do what they say they will. Many managers find themselves increasingly frustrated when team members fail to undertake the tasks we ask of them and spend unnecessary periods of time chasing up on forgotten jobs. One reason for this might be that the leadership style of the manager has 'switched off' the thinking in that person and there is a need to make a shift from a telling style to an asking style. However, it may also be because the manager hasn't pinned down the expectation clearly or specifically enough.

Pinning it down is a simple yet essential strategy for ensuring that people carry out the tasks of their role and is based around a few simple questions. On the bedrock of respectful, well-mannered, professional conversations, the leader agrees the task to be undertaken. This is the part that most of us do well: we articulate the job that needs doing and if we are good at this, we make sure the individual properly understands what we want them to do. However, if that's where we leave the conversation, we'll be living with the infuriation of some of our team not doing what they've agreed to.

To minimise this, we can continue the conversation for a brief period longer and ask some questions to consolidate and assure a satisfactory outcome. Once we've agreed the task and assured ourselves that this is understood, the question, "When will you do this by?" determines an agreed timeframe that the individual is now committed to. Then, "When will you feed back to me?" lets your colleague know that you expect them to tell you when it is done and how it went. It also facilitates accountability and responsibility to remain where it should be – with the person responsible for that task rather than with you as their manager.

If you want your teams to do what they say they will, pinning it down is a crucial part of your conversations. Next time you assign a task to someone, ask the 'pinning down' questions and then observe the outcomes. Check to see if a larger proportion of jobs get done without you needing to spend additional time chasing them up.

Feedback and Follow-through

Coaches won't complete their professional conversations at 'pinning down' point because this isn't the constructive final point of the intervention. It's all well and good agreeing and setting expectations with the coachee and asking questions to establish when it will happen and how they will feed back, but this isn't a cast-iron guarantee that the job will get done. Therefore, the professional coach will ensure feedback and follow-through.

Feedback is an essential component of coaching and it is two-way. The coachee is expected to feed back regarding the outcomes of their actions and the coach will feed back their observations for consideration by the coachee. This ensures mutual clarity about what is happening and whether intended outcomes have been achieved.

I am of the belief that feedback is one of the most crucial, valuable skills of any leader. I feel it is so very important that I've dedicated a whole chapter to it. We will tackle the detail of feedback in the Give the Feedback, Ask the Question chapter; suffice to say that if leaders don't seek feedback, how will they judge the standard and outcomes of their people? Mostly, we take on a responsibility ourselves to seek confirmation that tasks are undertaken, but how would it be if our teams fed back to us spontaneously instead? How much time would this save us?

The 'how will you feed back?' question from the 'pinning it down stage' requires follow-through to achieve a positive outcome. In my research of leaders, I have noticed that whilst we might be good at setting clear expectations and defining timeframes, we are not so good at following through. By following through I mean the action we take when things don't go according to plan. For example, let's suppose we agree a task with our team member and we pin it down to be done by a particular time and we also agree that they will report back on how it went by a particular date. We'll go about our own business in the knowledge that the task is all but done, but then a week later we suddenly realise we haven't checked and we haven't heard any more about it.

Cast your mind back and identify whether this is a familiar scenario for you: you spend valuable time running around, chasing information about tasks which you should have been able to trust to be done. What do you do about it? You add 'follow-through' to your leadership practice.

In order to encourage accountability and responsibility, there has to be a 'so what' consequence to our actions. This isn't a 'big stick' scenario, simply an understanding by all that when things don't happen as agreed leaders will follow through on it. They will have a conversation with their colleague to say, "We agreed this task by this time and you said you would feed back on this date, but I didn't hear from you. What happened?" This is a simple, respectful, adult conversation, based on questions, but it quietly delivers the implication that you expect people to do what they say they will. If they don't, you will notice and hold people to account – not in a heavy-handed way, but in an adult, professional way.

On a practical note, you will have to use an aide memoire, such as your diary, to reliably follow through – don't expect yourself to spontaneously recall everything you pin down with your team. This technique requires consistency if you are to sustain a culture where people take responsibility for their actions and do what they say they will. If you don't have follow-through, people will assume it's OK to not do things sometimes because there is no consequence attached to it.

Worse is where you tackle it with a 'telling off' which provokes a parent-child interaction; here accountability can be palmed off or ignored. There is never a reasonable excuse for managers to think they need to 'tell staff off'. Telling off is an unsophisticated way for leaders to tackle problems, which never has a positive outcome. Feedback and follow-through is the adult, professional option when things don't happen in the workplace in the way they should.

Experiment with follow-through. Next time you've pinned it down but the feedback doesn't come as you've agreed, make sure you have the conversation to find out why and how it will be rectified. Keep on having the conversations for as long as it takes – calmly, politely, respectfully and with conversation based on questions. Notice how quickly your teams will begin to realise they won't be let off the hook anymore for not doing what they've agreed to and how easy it becomes to hand back responsibility to where it should be held.

Throughout the past two chapters we have explored what coaches do and how leaders might 'borrow' coaching skills to incorporate into their leadership repertoire. Whilst at first glance there seems to be major work to do, if leaders take each experiment one step at a time, small changes begin to make a big difference.

Each of the skills discussed here are abilities which most people already have some proficiency with, it's just that we forget to translate them into everyday work habits. By working on each component, leaders can begin to engage with their teams better, encouraging responsibility and accountability in each individual, setting the tone for workplace interaction, and switching on the brain to ensure adult thinking and problem solving at its full capacity. These skills and shifts are the enablers for leaders to make the change from telling to asking.

CHAPTER SEVEN

The Problem with Taking on Problems

The previous section focused on the skills and attributes which coaches use to develop, change and extend the creative thinking capacity of the people they work with. These powerful interventions are invaluable for leaders who want to maximise the potential of their teams. They offer insight into the ways that leaders can change their behaviours to influence how people perform in the workplace and to ensure their staff can fulfil their roles with the maximum of thought and the minimum of parental-style supervision. They also offer practical methods of exhibiting love and care appropriately in work relationships.

I have suggested some simple experiments which leaders can try, to test out coaching skills within a leadership context. These will help managers to assess the value of behavioural shifts to the performance of their teams and provide evidence that improvements can occur with relatively small inputs. However, it is also important to recognise what coaches don't do, so that leaders can prevent themselves from falling into some common traps which can hinder team progress and development and create the opposite of the loving, successful, adult, solution-focused environments we would choose.

What Coaches Don't Do

The key to what coaches don't do is in the premise of the shift from telling to asking. In other words, coaches don't engage with 'telling' styles of behaviour because this impacts on the ability of another adult to think at their full capacity. After all, coaches need their coachees to be in 'thinking mode', otherwise development or change won't take place. Equally, leaders need their employees to be in thinking mode also because high standards, role fulfilment and problem solving stem from clear and constructive thinking.

Advice

A coach will never offer advice to their coachee unless as a very last resort when all other options, questions and lines of enquiry have been covered. Even then, a coach would only offer advice with the permission of the coachee, on the understanding that advice is the opinion of the giver of that advice, not the 'truth' or solution per se.

This flies in the face of what most managers believe their role is: to give valuable advice to their team as needed. When a member of your team comes to you with a problem or issue, your response is likely to be "Try this" or "Do such and such" or "I'd do X if I were you." These are our default responses because after all we are the manager and our job is to advise our people what to do, right?

There are two problems with giving advice as a matter of course. The first is that giving advice is a 'telling' action, which runs a heavy risk of inhibiting the thinking activity of the person to whom we offer the advice. Of course, we offer advice with the best of intention – because we want to help out and make sure that our people are equipped with all the information they need to do a good job. We interpret that 'helping' requires us to deliver advice so that our colleagues can move forward and be confident in doing things right.

But is interrupting the creative thinking potential of another individual actually helpful? It might be a quick way to sort the issue and it might make us as managers feel at our most useful, but is this really helping? What might be more valuable is an 'asking' intervention – a well-placed question which aims to 'switch on' thinking processes and abilities so that the person can create their own advice. The advantage of this is that it encourages our people to remain adult, resourceful and creative in the workplace. It discourages reliance and automatic deference to the perceived (parental?) 'wisdom' of the manager.

The second problem with giving advice is that we assume the advice we give is 'right'. We offer advice on the assumption that it is the right solution or answer to the problem. However, this is a precarious if not arrogant assumption. What we are actually saying is that it has, in the past, been the right solution or answer for ourselves, in a similar (but not exactly the same) situation, which is an altogether different thing. Because we tend to make universal assumptions – that a particular course of action worked for us before, for example – we presume it will be the same for someone else.

It couldn't possibly be of course; all we can hope to offer is something that once worked for us in a particular given context. This does not make it the 'right' answer, simply something that worked for us in that particular situation. Our people are not us, they are individuals with different views and experiences of the world. The danger of giving advice is that the world becomes all about us and what we would do; this inhibits creativity and individuality.

I am not suggesting that you should never give advice; there will inevitably be times when this is the best option. However, I am suggesting that rather than making advice your default position when someone has a problem or issue, make it your last resort. This will be incredibly difficult at first because it has become a habit; you may even feel like you're not being helpful when you first stop doing it. You may also get some strange reactions from your team; they will be in the habit of expecting you to tell them what you think or what they should do. However, this is a good thing; it is the first step towards enabling full thinking capacity in your people and encouraging adult thinking and working.

Replace your advice with questions. Find out more and ask them what they think, what they might consider doing differently, how they might work their own way through the issue. Offer support but not the (your) answers, be supportive of their thoughts and opinions even if they don't match your own. Providing someone isn't thinking of taking action that is illegal, dangerous or against company policy and procedures, who's to say that they won't come up with something even better than your potential advice in the first place? This is the route to innovation, change and creativity in teams, which can't be achieved if managers give advice as a first line intervention.

The Benefit of Experience

At the start of our discussion we acknowledged that good coaches don't necessarily require the same skill sets as those they are coaching. In fact, many coaches would say that it is beneficial not to have the same background and experience, as this allows the coach a more neutral view of the coachee's situation as well as facilitating questions from a place of interest and curiosity. Without too much prior knowledge, the coach can ask genuinely interested questions which won't lead the coachee because they aren't coloured by prior knowledge or preconceptions.

Positions of leadership, however, are generally the opposite of this. We are promoted to management positions because we display excellent knowledge and technical skills in our job roles and we are felt to have appropriate experience to move up the ladder and lead teams. It is no surprise then that we are keen to share that experience with others – indeed it would seem obvious that the role of a manager is to impart their experience.

Whilst this is an important part of managerial responsibility, sharing experience is a 'telling' interaction which carries all of the risks we have mentioned previously. It is not always of the benefit we might assume. Therefore, if we wish to create innovative, forward-thinking teams, we need to suppress our natural instincts to do so in the first instance. Adults are able to observe and process the behaviours of others – including more experienced colleagues. Therefore, if we hold back on disclosing the benefits of our experiences at first and ask questions instead, we maximise the ability of our people to process, analyse and work out what they might do. Questions might run in the form of, "What do you think is the right way? Have you ever seen anyone else deal with a similar situation? What did they do?"

Offering the benefit of experience is a vital component of leadership. However, as with advice, it isn't a universal 'truth'. The reality is that we might have been doing it wrongly or not in the optimum way ourselves without realising! Please give your teams the benefit of your prior knowledge and experience but do it with awareness so that you can do it well. Do it with the knowledge that you run the risk of disabling thinking and processing in others, so keep it short and only do it once you've asked enough questions to establish whether your colleagues need it or not.

Recommending that colleagues work in a particular way from your prior knowledge and experience isn't coaching, it's mentoring. Mentoring works at its best when staff are new to a role or situation and they don't yet know everything they need to know to do the new job well. However, this doesn't necessarily mean they know nothing at all. A good leader will ensure they find out, through questioning, what the new colleague already knows, then will share their knowledge and experience only to the extent that it is required. Knowing when to stop and recommence a coaching approach is key to maintaining capable, thoughtful people in your team.

Instruction

Instruction goes hand in hand with knowledge and experience; you can't teach someone something if you aren't relatively expert at it yourself. We often share our experience and knowledge through the process of instruction or teaching. A coach will never instruct a coachee – this flies in the face of the role they are undertaking. However, leaders may find themselves instructing and this can potentially be both positive and negative.

In a classroom sense, instructing is a valuable input. 'On the job' learning is also extremely powerful in helping people to extend current skills and learn new ones. We use teaching and training to help people learn new things in the workplace. 'How to' guides and instruction manuals are also key in organisations to assist people to work through procedures effectively.

However, to labour the point once more, instruction is a telling intervention – useful when people are learning new things but disabling if adopted as a routine communication style. Instruct sparingly, with awareness, so that you can do it well and achieve optimum results for your team without disabling their thinking and creativity.

Bringing it Back to You

We have already mentioned how ready we are to engage ourselves when people share anecdotes, problems or tales with us. Next time you're having a conversation, note how often you hear comments such as "Oh that happened to me once and I…" or "You think that's a problem, you should hear about mine…" or "Yes, but if you did this, or that, it wouldn't be a problem…" It is a natural, 'hardwired' response to want to bring the conversation to ourselves in dialogue – both inside work and outside.

A coach will very rarely give of themselves during a coaching session. If they did talk about themselves this would be a distraction for the coachee who may begin to seek or expect instruction and advice, inhibiting their own creative thinking. This is an incredibly difficult thing to stop doing because of our deep desire to bring our own opinions and experiences into the conversations we have. But what would happen if we could stop doing this?

Next time one of your team comes to discuss something with you, try to put every thought of yourself out of your head. Adopt an attitude that this is not about you, it is about them. Don't offer your opinion, advice, experience or instruction, just ask them questions. Allow the questions to come from a place of curiosity at first, to find out about and understand as much as possible what they're telling you. Practise attentive listening, then ask questions designed to get them to think their way through it, analyse, process and get creative about their next action. Their action – not yours!

Having an experience where you can talk, unhindered by someone else trying to hijack it with their own material, is a deeply satisfying experience. One might say it's a loving experience. It helps people to feel valued because someone else finds them interesting and important enough to take time to listen and focus solely on them and their issues. Coaches know that this sets the foundation for their coachee to explore deep and difficult issues. It also creates a sense of safety where people feel able to accept and deal with challenge and demand because they feel supported to do so.

This is a crucial element of leadership also. We need our people to learn to cope with the heavy demands and challenges of the workplace and to action them constructively and professionally. People can only do this if they feel supported, valued and important enough to face the difficulties. It isn't difficult for leaders to achieve this; we just need to stop bringing everything back to ourselves and focus on our people instead.

The Conversation Balance

We have all met managers who seem to love nothing more than the sound of their own voice. As managers ourselves however, we may feel that we need to lead by example, showing our teams and our bosses that we are competent and knowledgeable by doing lots of talking. We find ourselves explaining, sharing our thoughts, ideas and opinions – and if we are doing most of the talking, it must mean we know what we're talking about, right?

It won't surprise you by this point to know that coaches will keep their own talking to a minimum. With some thought, you will recognise that this is because if you are doing all the talking, you can't listen to anything. It's impossible to speak and listen at the same time. If they don't listen attentively, coaches can't ask appropriate, insightful or challenging questions.

Equally, if leaders do all the talking, it becomes all about them – their experiences, opinions and instructions. This creates the big 'switch off' in the brains of their teams, to a point where other people won't even be listening to what is being said. Savvy leaders, like great coaches, do more listening than speaking. When speaking does occur, it is mainly in the form of questions, to switch on the brains of others around them.

There is a great Buddhist teaching – that when you talk, you are only repeating what you already know; when you are listening, you are poised to learn something new. In my coaching work, I can honestly say that I have never walked away from working with someone without learning something new. I've learned new ways of approaching things; developed the ability to look at things from alternative viewpoints; learned different ways of practising and approaching situations; adopted new skills and tactics. These opportunities only come when you stop talking and listen more.

In leadership, learning from your team is invaluable. Presumably the people in your team are employed because of their skills and abilities to do the job. They'll also come with a whole host of background skills and experiences which might not be evident at first but which nonetheless make them who they are. It also makes them valuable to your team. You miss out on all the experience, knowledge and innovative potential of your people if you can't stop talking long enough to pay attention to them. You reflect that you don't care or value them enough to shut up and listen to their views and that only your voice is important. This is not a relationship which encourages loyalty and commitment in teams.

Great leaders (and coaches) always do more listening than speaking. Monitor how much you listen compared to speaking in your conversations. Unless you are formally teaching or instructing, you should aim for at least 60% listening to 40% talking, but preferably 70% - 30%. In specific 'thinking' contexts, such as appraisals or problem solving, you should really be aiming for 80% listening and 20% talking.

The Appropriateness of Emotion

The role of a coach is that of a neutral facilitator – a skilled individual who is impartial and who can therefore enable others to engage with self-identified issues and commit to self-identified actions. As a natural by-product, the coachee will inevitably experience a range of emotions and will express them to a greater or lesser extent during their coaching work. Emotions are a natural part of being human – we all come with messy emotions attached. Love is a particularly strong emotion of course.

Good coaches acknowledge this, expect it and encourage coachees to observe and deal with their emotions constructively. They don't 'infect' the emotions of others with their own because this complicates or shifts the focus of the work being undertaken by their coachee. Great leaders also recognise the value of this.

The workplace is different of course; as managers, we can't be wholly impartial, and we rarely feel 'neutral' about the things that go on in our areas of responsibility. We are also human beings who come with our own messy emotions attached. We want to express love and humanness through caring, compassion, respect and mannerly conduct. There is a plethora of literature arguing whether we should banish emotions from the workplace or embrace them wholly and you will hold your own views on this. Inevitably those views will be both personal and industry based; for example, we might be more tolerant of expressed emotion in a healthcare context than a corporate finance situation.

Whilst I take a 'middle ground' view of the emotion argument, I feel very strongly that there is a current trend towards being businesslike and professional, to the detriment of the human being in the workplace. I am the first to advocate for managers who are knowledgeable, committed experts in their field and who have a responsibility for ensuring the success of the organisation. However, those managers are human first and we can't pretend they are not. I worry that in our attempts to appear businesslike and value for money, we have 'over professionalised' our views and this has led to a denial that emotion – especially love – has a place at work. In turn, this leads to managers who are unprepared to deal with the destructive emotions which surge to the surface, after long periods of being suppressed in environments where emotion at work isn't tolerated.

Ideally leaders will function like coaches: expect emotions to be part of the human condition and enable people to express and control those emotions appropriately in the workplace. Coaches will set clear boundaries as to what is acceptable in the expression of emotions during work and will then facilitate the coachee to express and control emotion constructively.

Leaders do this first by example. I hear many stories of managers who feel it is acceptable to shout at others in the course of their work and do so regularly. I find this totally unacceptable – and I feel so strongly about that, I'm going to say it twice. It is totally unacceptable to shout at another person at work – unless the building is on fire or there is some other imminent disaster threatening their safety. At best, shouting at someone else is a parental action (inciting a childlike response) and at worst it is an uncontrolled, unprofessional, destructive display of emotion. If our managers are uncontrolled and disrespectful, what hope is there for anyone else?

Leaders who role model appropriate, controlled emotion at work are those who reflect value for the human aspect of their teams whilst balancing this with the needs of their service. Like coaches, they respect that we all come with emotions attached and they are unafraid to accept that there will be joyous as well as messy expressions of this because they are ready for them. They pave the way by articulating the boundaries of what is acceptable and what isn't and then model those boundaries through their own actions.

Great leaders (and coaches) recognise that uncontrolled expressions of emotion inhibit constructive working practices. None of us works well when we feel uncomfortable, humiliated or defensive around others. If we are shouting, we are most certainly not listening. If we are sarcastic or express frustration, we will create defensiveness in others; defensive people can't think productively and won't engage constructively with problems or issues.

Another issue of note is that of the 'jokey' manager. Sometimes we feel it is easier to make a joke of something than to tackle it seriously. However, it is rarely true that someone will seriously engage with a difficulty from a jokey approach; most likely they will treat it as a joke themselves, or they will feel too uncomfortable to be able to tackle it with any thought. For those managers who consider themselves to be a lovable comedian at work, beware. At best, your team will take everything you say light-heartedly and without substance; at worst you will be intimidating, tiresome and lacking in awareness of yourself and others.

Leaders can learn much from a coach's neutrality. Neutral doesn't mean unemotional – simply balanced and respectful of how our own emotion impacts on those around us. Balanced, positive emotion can be motivating and enhance wellbeing at work, but over-the-top positivity or hilarity creates discomfort and inhibits the significance of and sincerity towards important work requirements. Conversely, people need to know when we have negative feelings towards something in order to understand its seriousness and meaning; however, shouting, sarcasm and pseudo-jokiness inhibits constructive thinking and creates a defensive workforce.

Taking on the Problem

Coaches understand that when they work with their coachee – on problems, issues, new objectives or challenges – they do not 'own' or need to take on those areas of the work. In other words, ownership sits squarely with the coachee and the coach is not required to personally possess any attachment to them. Once mastered, this experience is often described as liberating: the ability to undertake constructive, profound work with another individual without needing to take on their problems or concerns as our own. In other words, the responsibility for the problem or issue remains with the person who owns it. Freed up from the problem, the coach is able to facilitate a deep level of work, unencumbered by the weight of the issue itself.

There is much to be learned from the neutrality of the coach, and if leaders liberate themselves from owning the problems of others, much deeper, more developmental work is possible. In his book *Shifting the Monkey*, Todd Whitaker uses a helpful metaphor in assisting leaders to understand the nature of problems and how they are best dealt with.

Whitaker describes the problems which crop up in the workplace as 'monkeys' and creates a picture of those monkeys attaching themselves to us or others. This becomes a problem when other people offload their monkeys to someone else when they should be taking care of them themselves. That person then becomes weighted down by monkeys which should be looked after by the people who are responsible for them. There is a notion that monkeys (problems) are needy – they need feeding and nurturing – so if one or just a few people are taking all the monkeys, the best, most hard-working people in the team will become jaded and burnt-out.

Shifting the Monkey focuses on how leaders should engage with team members who are constantly offloading their monkeys to other team members, or even customers. But what about those managers who routinely allow their people to offload monkeys on to them? Or worse still, managers whose default position in solving problems within their team is to take on and nurture everyone's monkeys as their own? No wonder so many managers become disillusioned and burnt-out.

I once worked with a senior nurse who led a team of qualified and unqualified care staff. She was so tired and disenchanted that she was considering leaving her career. It transpired that when her team were experiencing a problem or difficulty, they would take it to her to solve it. She would routinely take over the problem herself, at best offering advice on what they should do and, more usually, taking the problem away to solve herself. An example of this would be that a particular ward had run out of clean linen. She would go to the laundry herself to collect the clean stocks for the team.

The outcome of this was that she was so weighted down with monkeys that she had no time for her own responsibilities, so ended up working long hours to ensure her own job was completed. On top of this, her team were unable to solve even simple problems for themselves and relied on her entirely to take away their difficulties. They also called her outside of her working hours because they had stopped thinking for themselves.

Whilst her original intention had been to help her team, this senior leader had ended up so engaged with everyone else's problems that her input had disabled anyone from tackling their own monkeys. Her default position of giving advice had switched her team off from thinking for themselves and they had long since stopped bothering to tend to their own monkeys – she was so ready to simply take them on herself.

In this chapter, we have discussed what coaches don't do, to complement our learning from what they do. If leaders are going to be liberated from the weight of other people's monkeys, they must learn techniques to support their teams to hold and take care of their own problems. To do this, techniques of active listening, elegant questioning and excellent communication are practised in place of advice giving, experience sharing and a love of the sound of our own voices.

What we really need as leaders are teams of people who can come to work and do a great job. People who can engage with their responsibilities, solve their own problems and think productively and creatively. When our teams encounter difficulties, we need them to come to us and say, "I had a problem earlier and this is what I did about it…" rather than "Here's a problem…" followed by another and another.

It is essential that we reframe our view of helping our teams from taking over their monkeys to helping them to take care of their own. By leading in ways that switch on the brains of adults in the workplace we can ensure our team function to their optimum capability and also have the opportunity to grow and develop. The simple skills that coaches use are the vehicle to our achievements of this.

CHAPTER EIGHT

Questions, Questions and More Questions

We have discussed many skills and attributes so far that enable leaders to make a move from a telling to an asking style of leadership – all are important and come from a genuine place of care and respect for other people. However, by definition, if our leadership style is to be an asking one, we have to be skilled and confident at asking questions. Questions are those golden nuggets of communication that put the brain of the recipient into 'on' mode and ensures that people are ready to begin thinking and problem solving for themselves.

Just as a reminder, when one adult tells another adult what to do – in other words, when we give someone instructions, advice, opinions or statements – it inhibits the brain of that person from thinking for themselves. Every time you do this you will be powering down –

switching off – the ability of that person to think for themselves. You will also be creating a parent-child communication channel, which makes it even less likely that the person will take responsibility and function as an adult in the workplace. Every time someone comes to you with a problem, be prepared to support them in taking care of their own 'monkeys' rather than take it from them. Listening well is your first step to doing that, but the art of questioning is what will make you a master.

Just before we move on to the mastery of questioning, there is one caveat. Questioning is not a 'one size fits all' intervention; it should be your normal default position but not the only position you ever adopt. There are of course situations when this approach isn't appropriate, and these will normally be in crisis or emergency conditions. For example, if someone is in danger or there is an emergency such as a fire, you won't be gathering everyone round and asking what they think should happen next. You will take charge, be directive and fulfil your responsibilities as a leader, to ensure safety and minimise risk. However, the times when you need to lead like this will be very minimal indeed, although unfortunately, many managers function as if they're in an emergency all of the time.

Interestingly, if your default leadership position is to ask rather than tell, your teams will mobilise and respond much more quickly when you do need to be directive because the shift in your style will be bold and very noticeable. If you are a manager who is always directive, there will be less response from your teams because this is how you always behave – and you may find yourself having to shout and become overly animated in difficult situations to get people to take notice and respond. This is because their brains are in the 'off' position and they aren't prepared to think and respond quickly.

When you stop telling people what to do and ask more questions instead, your people will not only function to a higher standard every day, they will also respond much more efficiently when there is a crisis.

Sophisticated and Elegant Questions

Most leaders report that their biggest difficulty when making the change from telling to asking is knowing what questions to ask and having questions ready in their minds, so they don't have to flounder with the conversation. This will take practice, but if you have a sense of what makes a good question, alongside a small 'bank' of questions you know are useful, this will make the journey a little easier.

A question will always have more power if it comes from a genuine, authentic and caring place. Our original concepts of love and care are essential here. This is about the human respect and sincerity we offer to the person standing in front of us. If you can work from a bedrock of love and compassion, your questions will become honest and evocative in developing the thinking capacity of your people. You don't have to say this of course; what you say will be at its best if you keep it very simple. However, what you believe and feel in your gut will prompt the right question in the right moment. This is what forms the basis of a sophisticated question — not what you actually say, but the place it comes from and the intent with which you say it.

The less you speak, the more powerful the questions will be. Because we aren't used to questions, we tend to want immediate answers and we feel awkward if there is a little silence. Sophistication is about making silence your friend — it is a powerful moment to reflect for both yourself and the person you are speaking with. When there is quiet, the other person is thinking, and this gives you time to think also. Ask your question and then keep your mouth firmly closed!

Don't be tempted to ask another question or fill the space with chatter just because you feel a little uncomfortable. Offer up silent care and respect in support of the new thinking process the other person is starting to engage with.

Elegance in questioning comes from simplicity. Elegant questions are brief, broad and very simple. An elegant question won't try to lead someone in any particular direction or try to persuade someone to give a particular answer. They won't be long-winded or hide a suggestion or direction in the form of a question. Think short, clear and transparent, from a place of compassion and respect, and you will have a great question.

Starting to Question

There's a member of your team in front of you with a problem that really they should be considering and solving for themselves, and you are ready to make the shift from telling to asking. What do you do? You understand the concept of elegance and sophistication but what does that actually look like in practice?

The first principle to consider is that we don't often get the full information from the initial exchange we have with someone. What someone tells you will be their view, through their life filters and experiences. It will be complicated by your brain wanting to make assumptions about what you are also hearing from your filters and experiences. It is important you don't take the information at face value and you probe to get the most information you can. This is essential if you are going to stop wasting time chasing around issues that aren't the real or full story. Your time is valuable, so it's worth taking a few minutes to ask some questions and get the full story before you begin.

Your first questions should be focused on getting the maximum objective information possible and they look like this:

"Tell me more about that."

"What else happened?"

"What events led up to this?"

"How did this come about?"

"What are your/others' thoughts about this?"

"Has this happened before or is this the first time?"

You'll notice that all these questions are very short, and they are broad and neutral. In other words, they invite the person to give you as much information as possible, but they don't attempt to lead the answers, close down the conversation or lead it in any particular direction. As the conversation moves on, you will think of other questions you want to ask, relevant to the information you are getting. Remember, don't lead the conversation, avoid offering your opinions and experiences, and most importantly, don't be tempted to offer any solutions because this will inhibit the thinking and erase any steps the person has made to begin thinking for themselves.

Open versus Closed Questions

Questions can broadly be divided into two different types: open and closed. Open questions are those which encourage someone to give information and detail. They begin with words like What, How, Who, When, Where and Why. All of the example questions in the previous section are open questions because they all seek to elicit information and open out the conversation. Closed questions are those which require only a yes or no answer, so by definition they don't require the person to give lots of information or add detail to the conversation.

Much of the literature and advice on questioning suggests that open questions are much more effective than closed questions. In their training, counsellors and therapists are encouraged only to ask open questions and this is also true of some of the coaching literature and training. Whilst this is sound advice when we are looking to gain detail and information, open out the conversation and open up someone's ability to think, there are some instances when closed questions are very effective.

The human brain is a highly complex organ which continuously makes unconscious connections and interpretations from every sense and source. It makes such interpretations from the 'filter' of our views about life, our beliefs, learning and experience. This is a fantastic mechanism but it does have its downside. The problem is that our brain makes almost instant assumptions about what we hear, which can give us a false interpretation of what someone is saying to us. When someone is talking to us, we will actually hear only the first few words that are said, then our brain will make assumptions about the rest. In other words, we aren't actually hearing exactly what is being said, we are hearing our own brain's interpretation of it, from our own beliefs and experiences etc.

So closed questions are incredibly useful at making sure we are actually hearing what we think we are. They are essential in ensuring (so far as is possible) that we are taking on board information from another person as accurately as possible – from their perspective, not our own. It gives us a mechanism to check out that we have really heard what we think we have. Once you have asked open questions to gather information and detail about the issue, your closed, check-in questions might look like this:

"Am I right in thinking that…?"

"You seem pretty angry (upset/frustrated/happy etc.) about this. Am I reading that right?"

"So, what I hear you saying is…"

"My understanding of what you're saying is… Is that right?"

The final point about open and closed questions is the big issue about asking Why? On face value, this is of course an open question and it can be very powerful to ask someone why they did something, thought something or took a particular action. I would, however, urge caution when using Why? as an open question.

Your aim is to reflect care and genuine interest about people and asking questions is an act which does just that. However, Why? as a question is very easy to get wrong. It can come over as a harsh, parental, finger-pointing indictment if it's asked in the wrong tone or in an accusatory fashion. Go ahead and use Why? – it genuinely is very powerful in assisting understanding, but ask it softly and carefully to avoid defensiveness in the person you are asking. You are aiming to open up the conversation and enhance the understanding, not close it down.

Are There Right and Wrong Questions?

There aren't really right or wrong questions you can ask, just shades of grey and a few traps you might fall into. If your questions follow the sophisticated and elegant principles, you can't go far wrong but you will need to practise.

The easiest trap to fall into when starting out on the journey from telling to asking is to make a statement, give advice or try to lead the person into thinking what you're thinking, whilst wrapping it up as a question. These 'wrong' kinds of questions might look like this:

"Do you think that…?"

"Have you thought about…?"

"Why don't you…?"

"Did you try…?"

At first glance these are all questions and it's easy to think we've cracked it and are asking rather than telling, if we can put a question mark at the end of what we're saying. However, look again at the questions above – you may think of more like them. Really, they are opinions and advice, dressed up as a question. If you ask these, what you're really saying is 'I think this, and I want you to think it too'. If you do this, you're switching off the capacity of this person to think and work it through for themselves. You're only telling them what to do in a different way.

The questions above are leading and loaded. They are leading the person to agree with you and do what you want them to do, and they are loaded with instruction – you really are just telling them what to do. Your questions are right if they are neutral; this is not about what you think, it's about releasing the potential of everyone's thought and creativity, which will enhance your team and their performance. Avoid wrapping up an opinion or advice as a question.

Passing Back Responsibility and Being Creative

Once you have used questions to gather information and detail, and you have checked in with closed questions to ensure you have understood well, you are ready to move to the next stage. Don't rush this first stage though; it's vitally important to really get under the skin of it and that takes a group of questions and a bit of probing.

As I've mentioned before, the issue that someone comes to you with in the first instance is rarely the whole story. If you don't take the time to get the whole story and understand it from the other person's perspective, you run the risk of responding half-cocked or reacting to the wrong thing. This is a waste of your time! You might feel like you haven't got time to sit and ask a lot of questions, but I'm suggesting you will waste time unless you do just that. Spend your time working only on the real issues and problems, not the interpretation and assumptions of your brain. You can only do that if you take the time to probe and understand.

The next stage is to support the person to think, problem solve, find solutions and take action. No element of coaching is just about the chat – the crux is that you expect some action to be taken. This is business, not a cosy friendship, so care enough about your role and your business to get this right. Your questions here will remain elegant and sophisticated, but now they need to encourage creativity and empower others to take responsibility and accountability for themselves. Simplicity remains the key and the rule of silence and space to think becomes essential. Ask a question – just one at a time – and then offer time to think and respond. Don't jump in, even if there is an awkward silence. Your questions might look like this:

"What have you tried so far?"

This is an extremely powerful question, full of layers and implication. On a simple level, it says 'I trust you enough to take some sort of sensible action and I'm keen to hear about it'. If your team are used to being told and parented, this is a good way to start giving tacit permission to sort problems as they arise.

On a more complex level, if you have people who refuse to take responsibility or live up to the accountabilities of their role, this is a caring and respectful way of laying out your expectations. In other words, 'I expect you to have tried some actions before you come to me with this' is the unspoken implication. If you get into the habit of asking, "What have you tried so far?" your team will soon come to realise that they should attempt to solve problems before they come to you, providing the situation sits within their remit. If you use this question well over time, you'll soon have a team who say, "I had this problem, and this is what I did about it – just so you know" rather than simply unloading all the problems on to you.

Moving on from this, your aim is to develop creativity of thinking, so that your team find it easier to seek solutions and problem solve in the future. Questions like these may help:

"How do you think we should tackle this?"

"What are your thoughts about moving this forward?"

"What would you do next?"

"How might that happen?"

"Who could help you with this?"

"What else do you need to find out?"

"How could I support you to sort this out?"

All of these questions are caring, respectful and supportive, but leave the problem where it belongs – with the person who owns it. You will note they are all simple, non-leading and neutral, but they are open to encourage thinking and creativity, which will lead to responsible and accountable action. Don't be tempted to offer your own thoughts and opinions; this is not about you, this is about empowering the sensible adult in front of you to do their job to the highest possible standard.

Socratic Questioning

Go further to encourage creative and innovative thinking; when you start asking the questions above, the person will firstly give you their default position. As human beings, we tend to do what we've always done, so the solution someone gives you first will be their usual, everyday response. On some occasions this might be fine, but your aim is to open up the thinking of this person, empowering them to use their intellect fully so they can be the best possible version of themselves in their role. Having the opportunity for creative thinking is motivating and allows people to feel meaning and value at work. These are the things which improve attrition and encourage loyalty and 'going the extra mile'.

Aim to get the person to think differently than they might have done before – after all, if you always do what you've always done, you'll always get what you've always got. If you want to get different things, you have to do different things. If you want to do different things, you have to think different things. Your aim is to get some 'lightbulb' moments of thinking by asking questions and not necessarily taking the first answer but pushing until something different happens.

The thinking opens up and creativity starts to happen, then suddenly the person stops, takes a breath and knows that something has changed. They've come up with something different, thought something new that they wouldn't have done before. You can almost see the lightbulb light up over their head. This is Socratic thinking – the moment when you both know that something different has happened and thinking has moved somewhere new. You asked a question that changed the thinking pathway of that person and it moved somewhere else – a Socratic question.

You'll never know when you're about to ask a Socratic question and it won't happen in every single coaching conversation you have.

You'll absolutely know it when it happens though, and it will give both you and your team member a real buzz. It will happen when you're asking the questions in the previous section, but you don't let up after the first answer. You'll ask the question and then you'll probe:

"What else?"

"What other things can you think of?"

"What other advice might you give yourself?"

"And then…?"

"And after that…?"

"Anything else?"

Don't only ask these questions once, keep asking to push further and further into creativity and different thinking. It'll seem strange at first, but stick with it and it will soon become a way of triggering inspired and resourceful thinking in your team.

I Don't Know

Not everyone in your team will respond positively to being treated like an adult or being expected to behave responsibly and accountably in the workplace. This may be because they don't want to be responsible or accountable, but most likely it will be because they have learned to be dependent and childlike as a result of parental leadership styles. It might also be because some of your people are deeply reflective and need more time to think it through. If a lot of your team members resist your questioning, this is a sure sign of past autocratic and directive leadership experiences.

This will be learned behaviour and the good news is that people can unlearn old behaviours and learn new ones. You just have to persevere and be consistent with your new ways of working. People will come along with you at different paces – some quickly, some more slowly. Lots of people are likely to show resistance to some degree at first; exercise care and compassion, this is very new for them.

One of the most likely ways that people will reflect confusion or resistance is to say, "I don't know" or worse, "You're the manager, why don't you decide?" when you ask them a question. This can be incredibly disheartening when you've worked so hard to move from telling to asking and you've committed to the love and care of others in the workplace. It can feel like a kick in the teeth which has the potential to derail your leadership development and the potential of others around you. It will happen, so be prepared for it.

If you know a bit about how the brain works, you can be ready for some difficulty and challenge from your people. It is to be expected and is perfectly normal – after all, you're creating a new way of working for yourself and your team, which may be a real departure from anything experienced previously. Your understanding of it may be complex but your response and solution is very simple.

When we first receive information into our brains as a conscious process, it sits in the conscious, frontal areas of our brain where we think and process it in the moment. This part of the brain has capacity – it gets full up and we can only think about and process so many pieces of information at once. If we're used to being told what to do, it's also the part of the brain that stops thinking and processing in response to a telling approach.

The rear, more primary and subconscious parts of our brain are now thought to be infinite in their capacity to think and problem solve. These are the areas that continue to work through issues and problems when we are not consciously thinking about them. It is widely agreed that these parts of the brain can't not problem solve – in fact they carry on processing things when we're occupied with other things or even sleeping. You know this to be true instinctively because we've all experienced the results. It's this process in action when you suddenly wake in the night and remember where you've left your car keys; or you are watching TV in the evening and you suddenly recall the name of the person you spoke to on the street earlier. Our brains have carried on working on the problem whilst we have consciously stopped thinking about them and then the solution has been released into our conscious brain.

Knowing this brain science is your battle plan – it will help you to continue your journey from telling to asking, even when someone responds with "I don't know." Should this happen, don't be disheartened. Use the brain science to encourage the brains of others to do what they do best – think and problem solve. It sounds complex but it's actually very easy; you simply have to ask more questions, although this time with a little more suggestion or direction attached. It remains neutral still and looks something like this:

Team member: "I don't know."

You: "OK, don't worry, why don't you go and have a think about it? Let's meet up again this afternoon (tomorrow/next week etc.) and see what you've come up with then."

At this point you will stop talking and move away; this is very important because you want the issue to move from the conscious brain to the subconscious. You need the person to go away and allow their enormous capacity for thinking and problem solving to take over. The longer you keep them talking about it, the less likely this is to happen.

When you meet up with them again, they will very likely come back with some thoughts and solutions, particularly if they are reflective and have appreciated some time to think. There may still be some people here and there determined not to participate, but persevere and remain consistent. The message is clear: you are all developing to reap the benefits of collaborative and facilitative working.

Pin It Down and Follow It Through

In everything that leaders do, the message of pin it down and follow it through is absolutely crucial. Unfortunately, it is also one of the things we do least well. You can have the best coaching conversation in the world, ask the most elegant and sophisticated questions, reach the most innovative actions and solutions, but unless you are clear about what will happen and when and how you will receive feedback and review, your work will likely be wasted.

Once you have agreed the action which your team member will take, following a successful question-based interaction, you will ask some final questions to pin it down and follow it through:

"My understanding of what you plan to do next is… When will you do that by?" (get a specific, realistic date/time)

"How will you feed that back to me?"

"When should I expect that by?"

Don't end your conversation until you have a commitment, otherwise it's unlikely that any action will be taken, especially at first. If your team member doesn't come back to you voluntarily, go to find them and ask about it. Don't get upset if they didn't do anything – this is new, and they've likely got away with doing nothing because follow-up didn't happen before. If you're consistent, they will soon get the message that you expect everyone to do what they say they will and you'll follow it through if you don't get feedback. If nothing got done, ask more questions:

"Let's talk about why that didn't happen."

"What stopped you?"

"Is there anything else you need?"

Then pin it down again and follow it through – as many times as it takes to get the message over that things happen differently in your team now. Keep asking the questions and keep following through.

In this chapter we have explored the art of questioning. It is most definitely an art – a skill which, with practice, you can master and incorporate into your everyday leadership behaviour. It is the key to the shift from telling to asking and will ensure you empower the full capacity of your team. I would encourage you to stay alert for great questions – you'll hear them and use them yourself and you'll come to know which are most likely to bring results and create Socratic thinking in others. Write them down and use them often and then over time, wait to hear your team using them around you, with each other. This is when you'll know you're a true questioning master.

CHAPTER NINE

Give the Feedback, Ask the Question

When I'm training leaders to lead using collaborative and facilitative styles – the Coaching for Leadership approach – feedback is a pivotal topic. I often say to the managers in the room that if there is only one message they have the capacity to take away from the module, I would choose it to be this. Of course, I hope they take away much more – everything the learning has to offer. I hope you too find many things of use as you work your way through this book. But this is such an important message and this chapter offers one of the most fundamental skills a leader can master, in my opinion. It is a core set of skills on which the Coaching for Leadership approach is built.

By the end of the chapter I hope you will see 'Give the Feedback, Ask the Question' as a mantra. Something you say over and over to yourself, sure in the knowledge that it is a fast and focused tactic which captures the Coaching for Leadership premise in one swift action.

As you are learning the shift, there will be periods when you feel genuinely concerned that you don't have the time to make a switch from telling to asking. You are madly busy, there are more targets than there are hours to meet them and it seems that you only have time to give directions and hope for the best that your team follow them. How could you possibly take the time to sit, listen attentively and ask questions instead? I have two aims for this chapter, other than to make you a Give the Feedback, Ask the Question champion. The first is to convince you that if you invest a little time, you will reap it multifold down the line; secondly, that it doesn't need to take as long as you might think.

Feedback as a Core Skill

I'm often asked by leaders what are the most important skills we need to have to be the most excellent manager we could possibly be. That's a tough question and I would say there are a few, which will change in priority with changes in circumstances. However, the one thing always in my top three is the ability to give great feedback. This seemingly simple talent is much underused in the workplace but is incredibly influential in ensuring our teams deliver exactly what they're supposed to, to the highest possible standard. It's also fundamental if we want to ensure their brains are in the 'on' thinking position and our teams are prepared and supported to be as highly functional as possible.

Unfortunately, much of what takes place on a day to day basis in our teams is based on assumption. We assume that all of our people know exactly what to do, to what standard; that they're fully conversant with their job description, having the right skills for everything they are responsible for. Alongside this we assume that all of our people also have some awareness of the role and responsibilities of others in their teams, the people around them with whom they interact and also of us as leaders.

I'm not suggesting these are inappropriate assumptions – of course we have robust induction and on-boarding strategies; we support our people through appraisal and supervision; and there is ongoing training, learning and support. These are all aimed at equipping our people to do the job well. Despite this, almost everyone I speak to can identify team members, past or present, who come to work and don't do everything as expected. They are the 'difficult' individuals, or the ones who no one else wants to work with because they are 'too slow' or 'don't care' or are 'lazy' (or any number of other perceived reasons). The interesting thing is that whatever the perception, everyone knows who they are – except the person themselves. The other interesting point is that these people are rarely newbies, they are employees who have been in the team for years; likely, they've also been doing a mediocre job for years.

I am a firm believer that no one gets up in the morning planning to do a bad job. No one's first thought when they wake up is 'I know, I'll just go to work and do a really second-rate day's work today'. Except there are thousands of people who arrive in the workplace and do exactly that. Why is this? My experience is that it's mostly because those employees have no idea that they aren't functioning as well as everyone else. You might disagree with me, but if they've been told about their performance, reflect on that. Told? In a way that shuts down thinking capacity rather than supports insight and problem solving? The other piece of the agenda is follow-through. If you are sure the person is aware of their unacceptable performance, so what? Is there follow-through and consequences, or does that person think it's OK to carry on because nothing will happen anyway?

Human behaviour is pretty consistent in this area. Let's just imagine that you've worked in your job for several years, doing the work as you always have, in the same way, and no one says to you 'actually that's not how we do things around here', what will you think? You will of course think that everything is fine. After all, if no one says it isn't fine, our natural default position as a human being is to assume that everything is right and good. We will carry on in the sure knowledge that all is well. Even if someone did mention that one or two things about our performance weren't great, we will carry on regardless if that's never mentioned again, or followed through, or no one seems to care whether we change our behaviour or not. This is normal, natural, human default behaviour and it will almost always play out this way.

The solution is about leadership and more specifically about the ability of leaders to give great feedback – good and bad, many times a day, as a normal feature of daily leadership behaviour. I can almost hear you groaning again, 'yet another thing to add to my already packed agenda'. Please be reassured – the techniques discussed here will create time, with a little upfront investment. This is because with the addition of great feedback to your repertoire of skills, your team will almost certainly up their game and get on with their jobs, to a higher standard, even when you're not there. My research also suggests that for the rare few who totally resist upping their game, they are much more likely to move on, and their moving on will come from their own choice, in a non-confrontational, non-formal way.

This happens because great feedback comes from a place of love, care and respect. You can deliver it in a forthright and honest way because of this. If you learn to do it well and you incorporate it as a normal part of your daily conversations with your team, they will know that you mean it and you will follow up on it. If you deliver it from a Coaching for Leadership premise, you will open up their brains to think about it constructively, so they will find ways to improve and meet expectations that are meaningful to them.

The techniques are also simpler and much faster to implement than you might think. I'm not talking about lengthy conversations behind closed doors which take you away from getting on with the business of the day. These are interactions in passing which take seconds once you've learned the technique. They are frequent, normal, day to day observations which you will make verbally on your normal walks around the business or the normal daily interactions you have with your teams. If you speak with people in the normal course of your daily work and leadership, you can learn to give great feedback and reap enormous benefits in the performance of your people.

What Makes a Great Piece of Feedback?

Most of us are pretty skilled at identifying what good feedback is, but it doesn't hurt to revisit and develop thinking around such an important topic. Great feedback isn't positive or negative – it's both. As leaders we need to give positive as well as negative feedback, very regularly, to all members of our teams. At first, this will seem strange – to you and them. However, habits quickly form and become a way of life, so stay consistent and persevere; the experiment here is to observe what changes in your team when you adopt a feedback approach. Despite what you may think, most of your team will be doing most things well, so unsurprisingly you should expect there to be more positive feedback than negative. Both are essential if this technique is to work at its best though. The aim is to get used to feeding back on everything you see.

It makes no difference whether you are delivering feedback about positive performance or highlighting things that you do not want to see, performance-wise; the components of a great piece of feedback are the same. Reflect for a few minutes on what you know makes a well-delivered piece of feedback. Write some notes and see what you come up with.

The easiest way to identify the components of great feedback is to place yourself on the receiving end of feedback from your own line manager, in your mind's eye. Imagine you were at work yesterday and something didn't go quite to plan – something went wrong, or you made a mistake with something. You didn't make a mistake intentionally of course – as I mentioned above, no one does. However, bad things happen and when they do, they need to be acted on and followed through. Your line manager calls and says they need to have a conversation with you regarding what went wrong. It's feedback time!

How would you like to receive that feedback? Reflecting deeply on that will help you to tease out the components of a great piece of feedback because you almost certainly won't want to receive it differently from anyone else on the planet. Human beings appreciate being spoken to in particular ways, regardless of their role, title, status or anything else – because they're human! I have carried out this exercise with many hundreds of managers and the results are incredibly consistent, whether I'm working with 'C' or 'D' level managers or team leaders and supervisors. They have all reflected on how they would like to receive feedback, and this is what they come up with:

Private – without exception, we all want to receive feedback in private. Who would want their boss to have a conversation with them in front of other people about something which has gone wrong? Public feedback conversations do nothing to facilitate adult, constructive, respectful dialogue. We all know this, yet I'm always astonished to hear how many managers continue to think it's acceptable to do it publicly. It is not – end of! Managers who do are likely exercising power and status to get something done rather than applying skill in developing their teams to reflect and work better. An even worse notion is that managers give feedback publicly to 'make an example'. If you could ever get to the opposite end of the spectrum from leading with love, care and respect, this would be it. No one needs to be made an example of – this is unskilled, unsophisticated and inhuman leadership. You will absolutely always get better results from your people if you always deliver feedback privately.

Our context so far though is when a mistake or problem has occurred and feedback needs to be given. Is this the same when we're offering positive feedback? Reflect on your thoughts about this for a moment. My own view is that privacy still applies. We might think that it's helpful for everyone to hear when things have been done well, but you may be shooting yourself in the foot by delivering the feedback publicly. Many people feel embarrassed by being praised in front of others – this may be a cultural or learned thing; also, if your teams aren't accustomed to receiving feedback, you may unwittingly cause cliques or problems if it triggers a 'teacher's pet' mentality. My suggestion is to give the positive feedback privately, then seek permission to make it public if you see benefits of doing so.

The First to Know – if our line manager has something to say about our performance, it's personal to us and we should always be the first to know. There's nothing worse than receiving a piece of feedback and then finding out that other people knew already. Unless something is illegal or life-threatening, feedback is personal in the first instance, so give it first to the person who owns it. If you're tempted to discuss it with someone else first, ask yourself why. Guard against just reassuring yourself; if you know how to give a great piece of feedback, you shouldn't feel the need to get reassurance. If you are skilled and confident to allow the owner of the feedback to be the first to know, you will engender respect and loyalty because that person will know instinctively that you come from a place of love and care.

Confidential – this relates in an overarching way to the above two points. We all understand about confidentiality and data protection in a legal, safety and technical sense, but in many organisations this seems not to relate to actual human beings. You can exercise absolute privacy in your conversations and always ensure that the owner of the feedback is the first to know, but if you then tell someone else, who tells someone else, that feedback owner is going to hear it at some point. Your credibility will be lost in an instant and any loyalty and respect will vanish. If you want to lead like you give a damn, confidentiality is a crucial component of workplace conversations. Uphold it totally at all costs.

Timely – when is the best time to receive a piece of feedback? The answer is now; feedback is most powerful in the moment it happens, or as soon as possible after the situation has happened. This is when the brain is at its most ready to consider and reflect because the issue is in the conscious, processing zone. I'm always appalled when I hear managers saying that they'll feed back to someone 'at their appraisal next month' or 'at their supervision in a couple of weeks' time'. Feedback needs to be given now, so if you're not giving it now, ask yourself why. It's mostly because it makes us feel awkward, even if it's positive and praising, so we put it off. We imagine that there will be discomfort and confrontation, or even that people might not like us anymore. The reassurance is that if you learn exactly how to give a great piece of feedback, you'll feel confident, you'll avoid any difficulty or embarrassment and you'll feel able to deliver it as it should be – as something developmental and respectful.

Timely is of course related to privacy – so if you can't create the privacy, leave the conversation until the earliest moment that you can.

Calm – this is usually one of the first points about feedback that very senior leaders come up with, which I find very interesting. When

I mention it to middle and supervisory leaders, they also agree of course; but the worrying thing is, they're so used to being yelled at and on the receiving end of disrespectful conversations, they don't even think it worth mentioning. We have a situation where senior leaders want it, but on the face of it, that's not what they're dishing out to their teams. Calm is a vital component of love, care and respect. If you aren't calm when you're giving feedback, you will never give it well and you are disrespecting yourself and the people you talk to. You might make the defence to yourself that you're just being passionate, but stop making excuses. Unless the building is on fire or there's a life-threatening situation, I can't think of any reason that one adult would think it's acceptable to shout at another adult in the workplace – *ever*.

This aspect will also impact on your ability to give feedback in a timely way. You're a human being too and you come with emotions attached. Inevitably there will be times when someone in your team will do something that makes you feel angry, frustrated, disappointed or whatever. This is normal and natural, but it will get in the way of helpful conversations. If you're so angry you feel like tearing into someone, please don't give feedback now. Calm down and then deliver it as soon as you are composed again.

Adult – this is an interesting component because what makes a feedback conversation (or any conversation for that matter) adult? All of the above contribute to an adult approach of course, but it's more than that. It's a shift in approach, attitude and languaging of the situation. One of the things I'm always most concerned about is when managers tell me that part of their role is the 'telling off' of their team when they do something wrong. Think about that for a moment: what does it say when one adult thinks they have to 'tell off' another adult? If this is part of your language and the language of your organisation, there is work to be done to shift to an adult stance in the workplace.

'Telling off' is a parental activity, which will incite childlike behaviours in others as a result. No one should tell off anyone else in the workplace. Feedback, given well, is the skilful, sophisticated, adult alternative to 'telling off' which inspires development, constructive consideration and solution finding in others.

Constructive – this component follows on from adult. Most of us identify that if we've made a mistake, we want the opportunity and freedom to do something about it; to put it right or do it better. Great feedback allows opportunity for discussion, negotiation, creativity, action and follow-through. This isn't just a 'deliver and run' situation; follow it through to the end and respect people enough to find a way to put things right.

Straight – I've never met anyone who says 'give it to me dressed up and pink and fluffy'. If we're going to be on the receiving end of feedback, the vast majority of us want it straight. Don't beat about the bush or dress it up as something else – that just creates more anxiety and more uncomfortable anticipation of what is to come. Say it as it is, clear and straightforward. It's what everyone would opt for.

There is much written about the 'feedback sandwich' style of offering feedback. This was once the go-to method of giving feedback: start with something positive, hit them with the difficult stuff in the middle and then finish on something positive. The evidence now points to the fact that it doesn't work. It's too complicated, takes too long and people don't always hear the true message you're trying to give them. If you've got something positive to say, say it. If you've got something negative, just be clear, adult and respectful with what you have to say, and you won't go far wrong.

Behaviour is all there is – there is only one thing you should ever be giving feedback about in the workplace and that's behaviour. And I do mean ever! Most of our difficulties with feedback stem from the fact that we're trying to comment on things other than someone's behaviour. You'll get into deep water if you make observations and judgments about esoteric things like attitude, beliefs or hearsay. The very best feedback is only about behaviour and ideally delivered by the person who observed it, at the time they observed it. Good and bad.

Your role as a leader isn't to like people, make judgments about their personalities or quash differing opinions. It's to make sure the job gets done, to the right standards and expectations. Behaviour is what's measurable, observable and it's also something people can change and improve. Feedback is so much easier, more respectful and more constructive when you can say, "I notice that you're ten minutes late again today and it's the third time this week" rather than, "Your attitude to timekeeping stinks and you're letting everyone down." Think about the difference in response you might get to each of those statements. Make it easier for yourself and your people to do well; focus on behaviours you can measure and change, not judgments which create controversy and conflict.

Delivering Great Feedback

I'm pretty confident that if you sat for a while reflecting on great feedback, you would have come up with all of the above components: privacy, first to know, confidentiality, timely, calm, adult, straight, constructive and behavioural, or at least derivatives thereof. If you stick to those rules, you won't go far wrong, but that still doesn't give enough specifics of exactly **how** you do it and just as importantly, how you do it quickly and efficiently.

With all of those components in mind, there are a couple more rules to follow when giving great feedback:

Short and Simple – we covered this mostly in the 'straight' section, but I want to point you more precisely. Great feedback is sophisticated in its simplicity. The more straightforward you make it, the faster it is to deliver and the fewer opportunities there are for misunderstandings. To do this really well, you must get into the habit of giving feedback frequently to your team. Habitual feedback allows you to cover only that aspect of the moment. This ensures you are only discussing one issue at any one time – it's fast, focused and efficient that way. It means you can deliver feedback covering all the essential components in a minute or less.

Every Hour, Every Day, All of The Time – this is probably the hardest habit for leaders and their teams to form because it feels so contrived and alien at the beginning. It means that every time you walk around your service, interact with your people or observe performance, you should seek opportunities to give a piece of feedback. The goal is to become accustomed to giving and receiving feedback all the time – create a culture of feedback, which in turn creates an aware, open and accountable workforce. It's surprisingly simple to do, providing you commit to it and don't get put off by the surprised and confused reactions of your people as they try it out for the first few times.

Every time you come across another human being, look for opportunities to give feedback – good and bad, but the good should always outweigh the bad in volume. All you have to do is comment on what you see, following the rules of great feedback.

More of the Good and Less of the Bad – it's essential to consider why you are giving feedback and why it's so important. The answer is simple, and it's related to the reason why we're leaders and managers in the first place: we manage so that our people, service and business are the best they can possibly be. We can achieve this by giving great feedback because at the bottom line, feedback is about getting more of the good stuff and less of the bad stuff from everyone. In order to do this, people need to know exactly what the good stuff is and exactly what they should do less of – in detail.

They also need to know that their manager looks for it, feeds back on it and follows through on the outcomes, good and bad. In other words, they need to know that their manager cares – about them and the business. Great feedback allows you to do this.

State the Obvious – we often put off giving feedback because we can't find the right words to say it. Offering praise and positive feedback can be slightly easier, although we still flounder with it and more so when we need to offer criticism, no matter how constructive. But all you have to do is observe the behaviour and say what you see. Make a short statement of the obvious, that's all. You work with adults who have the capacity to think. To get more of the good and less of the bad, all you have to do is bring one or the other to their attention, as it happens, in a straightforward manner and then allow them to give it some thought. The key is just to make a statement of exactly what you see – just the behaviour, just state the obvious.

Neutral and Unemotional – the single, most damaging act when you're giving feedback is to bring it loaded with judgment and emotion. This is what causes difficulty, controversy, conflict and ultimately those dreaded complaints and grievances – all of the most powerful reasons why we avoid giving feedback in the first place. If you stick to the golden rules of state the obvious, about the behaviour, in a neutral and unemotional way, you'll avoid all of that.

I'm not suggesting you shouldn't feel angry, frustrated or upset, but you really do need to keep those things out of what is said. The less you say and the simpler it is, the easier that will be. If you make your feedback statements long, complex and detailed, you're less likely to achieve it well. Sarcasm, irony or making a joke of it is a poor way to get more of the good and less of the bad. Stay neutral and unemotional and you will reap the rewards.

How Great Feedback Looks

If you look back over this chapter so far, you might find it easy to think that I wasn't being truthful when I said this is a fast and efficient way of engaging with your people and getting them to be responsible and accountable. The act of feedback itself is fast but you have to launch it from a foundation of love and care. You need to know all of the above to do that and here is what it looks like in action.

The act of delivering feedback itself takes a simple few seconds. All you have to do is observe the behaviour, then ensure no one else is within earshot before you speak. Don't make it cloak and dagger, behind closed doors stuff – you don't have time for that. Just make sure you can't be overheard or overlooked too obviously. Then simply say what you see, without judgment or emotion. That's all.

Here are a few scenarios to illustrate how it looks:

It's the middle of the working week and one of your team is late again. It's the third time this week; targets are beginning to slip, and everyone is grumbling about it. You're feeling frustrated, but you don't want to cause an argument when things are so busy. The feedback is: "*I notice you're ten minutes late Bob. It's the third time this week.*"

You walk into a public area in your workplace and you overhear one of your team members raising his voice to a customer. No one else has noticed, but this is potentially risking customer relations and your reputation. You wait until you have the team member in a private place and then you give feedback: "*I overheard you raising your voice to a customer.*"

You are walking through the business and you notice an employee dealing really productively with a difficult and challenging client. You wait until the interaction is over and you are in a quiet spot and you give the feedback: "*I saw you were working really productively with Mr Smith and how positively you were able to help him.*"

I hope these examples help you to see that whilst the premise of feedback is rigorous, the act of delivering it is very simple. The aim is simply to point out what is going on so that people can act to improve or continue the behaviour. As a result, they will know exactly what you want more of and precisely what you want to see less. When you make a simple feedback statement, you are prompting the brain of the individual into the 'on' position, where thinking, reflection and creativity can commence.

Feedback Plus – Supersize Your Feedback

If you stop at just the feedback, you will have a team who begin to know what you want and what you don't. In itself it's productive and transparent and allows a constructive way for you to talk with your people all the time. However, there is more you can do. Our aim is to get the maximum output from your feedback investment.

So how do you push it forward? Offering a great piece of feedback will ensure your team member's brain is poised for thought, reflection and problem solving. You will have prepared the ground for further opening out of their thinking capacity and they will be primed for creativity and development. A couple more skilled, simple interactions from you will achieve that and it will only take a few more seconds.

The Power of One Second

In order to expand the feedback into an adult, constructive conversation with development potential, you need to fire up the brain of your team member now. You have caught their attention in a calm, respectful manner and you have implicitly let them know that this is important, and you are going to follow it through. In the end, the simple approach is the more sophisticated one and stating the obvious, saying what you saw without judgment and emotion, has ensured you get to be constructive in moving it forward, without having created conflict or defensiveness.

To get the best from the other person, you now have to shut up. Stop talking, stay silent. One second of silence is all it will take but expect it to feel difficult, at least at first. One second of silence can seem like an eternity in a world we're so determined to fill with noise, but it's vital to creating creativity and development. Deliver the feedback in a short, simple statement, then be quiet for one whole second.

In that second, you give your team member some valuable thinking time. You also infer they are an equal, important part of this conversation and they are invited to contribute. Most importantly though, you are triggering action, not just contemplation. The neuroscience evidence suggests that in order for someone to take action – to do something different – they have to feel a mild state of discomfort. This tips over the neural functions of the brain from thinking mode to action mode. The emphasis is on mild because great discomfort causes paralysis and lack of action.

One second of silence is all it takes for a person to feel mildly uncomfortable, particularly if it comes after a feedback statement. They are now much more likely to do something, take some action rather than disregard the feedback. This is what you're after – feedback is about people performing differently – getting more of the good stuff and less of the bad. You may get babbling, excuses, apologies or just silence back – all are normal responses and to be expected. All you have to do is listen attentively or tolerate the mild discomfort you may also feel in that moment of silence. Don't fill the silence yourself, whatever you do. After one second, you're ready to move on and supersize your feedback.

Give the Feedback, Ask the Question

With the creation of a mild sense of discomfort, the brain of your team member is ready for creativity and action. Your goal is to make your feedback make a difference. You want to optimise the opportunity to grow and develop your people and therefore make your service the best it could possibly be. So now you ask a question.

You already know that the power of asking a question is profound. Shifting from telling to asking enables people to use their full brain capacity to think, reflect, develop and act. This is how you keep the problem – the monkey – where it should stay, but with your support and care. You ask a question because you give a damn about how this turns out and you want it to be good. Make your question short, simple and sophisticated. If your team member responds with "I don't know", don't fret about it, just send them away to think about it and be sure to follow it through later. They will almost always be more constructive and sensible than you anticipate.

This is what Give the Feedback, Ask the Question looks like in practice:

"I notice you're ten minutes late Bob. It's the third time this week."

Stop talking and make one second of silence.
Listen to anything the person has to say then ask a question:

"How are you going to ensure you get here on time from now on? How can I help you with that?"

"I overheard you raising your voice to a customer."

Stop talking and make one second of silence.

Listen to anything the person has to say then ask a question:

"It's concerning to hear anyone shouting at a client; what was happening?"

"I saw you were working really productively with Mr Smith and how positively you were able to help him."

Stop talking and make one second of silence.

Listen to anything the person has to say and then ask a question:

"This is great work; how do you think we could get the rest of the team to do that? How do you think we could share the learning with the rest of the team? Would you mind if I shared this with the team so we could all learn from it?"

'Give the Feedback, Ask the Question' is a powerful mantra. If you use it 10, 20, 100 times a day, every day, you will start off with a puzzled team; move on with a team who see exactly what you want more and less of and who know you are going to follow things through; and end up with a team who are fully accountable and responsible within their roles whether you are there or not. They will feel respected, valued (loved and cared for) and you will be able to challenge and develop them fully because of it. If you are really lucky, you will create a team who go on to feel skilled and confident at giving each other – and you – ongoing feedback, which will further enhance and optimise performance. Don't take my word for it, do the experiment. Give the Feedback, Ask the Question often. Practise, persevere and observe the impact, you have nothing to lose and everything to gain. Give the Feedback, Ask the Question is the epitome of loving to lead.

CHAPTER TEN

Using Coaching for Leadership to Manage Marginal Performance

This whole book is about managing performance – your own and others'. You can't deliver a great service, at any level, without delivering on great performance. That's what Coaching for Leadership is all about; at a very detailed level, it's Give the Feedback, Ask the Question. What we're considering in this chapter is that 'grey' area of performance that's so difficult to manage because it's vague and insidious. It's not so horrendously bad that you have no choice but to implement relevant HR policy and procedure, but it's not good and it certainly isn't what you want to accept from your people.

This area of marginal performance is extremely difficult for leaders to manage. It's very difficult to pin down, describe or act on because by very definition it's borderline. Take one episode on its own and it's negligible, but over time, many incidences of minor poor performance begin to become highly problematic.

People notice poor performance because it impacts on team function insidiously. Standards drop and people who are performing well can become demotivated and disheartened because they seem to be doing all the hard work and others are allowed to bring it all down. You find it extremely hard to tackle but you can't not – if you let it go, you're implying it's OK. What does saying it's OK do to your reputation and the standards of your service?

Unfortunately, because marginal performance is so difficult to articulate and deal with, we either use a 'sledgehammer to crack a nut' approach, or we disregard it until it becomes so bad we must implement formal disciplinary procedures. Neither is helpful, developmental or uses your time and resources efficiently. The other difficulty is lack of confidence. Leaders who lack sophisticated, collaborative and facilitative skills tend to reach for formal HR policies and procedures as a first action and then wonder why they don't have trust, loyalty and accountability from their teams.

I'm not saying that formal procedures don't have their place, of course they do. But if leaders can employ a skilful Coaching for Leadership style, the incidences where these are necessary are far fewer. This is because incidences of marginal performance become fewer because people are clearer about what you want more of and what you want less of.

I often hear leaders discussing their 'difficult' team members. Invariably they are people in teams who sit in the 'marginal' performance category and they take up a huge amount of management time. Over time, we begin to say, "This has gone on long enough, I need to performance manage them now." But what do we mean by this? Performance manage them? In my book, managing performance is the day job of every leader. It's the core of any leadership role; it's the minute by minute behaviours a leader displays to get more of the good stuff and less of the bad. So, shouldn't you be managing performance in every member of your team all of the time?

I do of course realise that when we say 'performance manage' someone, what we're really saying is implement formal performance review procedures; but wouldn't it be nice if we could avoid that? You'll never avoid it in its entirety of course, that would be unrealistic; but I passionately believe that if you lead collaboratively using a Coaching for Leadership style, with Give the Feedback, Ask the Question your most frequent interaction, your incidences of marginal performance will reduce drastically.

The Absence of Feedback, Questions and Follow-through

We have spent a great deal of time so far looking in detail at the skills of feedback, questioning and follow-through, as well as the essential ability to listen attentively. It's often useful in understanding the origins of marginal performance to consider what happens in the absence of leadership capability in these areas. In other words, could it be possible that to some extent we might initiate marginal performance ourselves, through a lack of collaborative leadership skills?

Saying Thank You

When I ask leaders how their staff know they are appreciated, they usually tell me that they always make sure they say thank you. This is a key factor of appreciation – very simple and very important.

You might even argue that it's how you show appropriate love in the workplace – that you care about and respect the work that others do. However, do your teams know what you're saying thank you for? We have discussed the premise of getting more of the good things and less of the bad as a core function of managing performance, so exactly what message are you giving when you say thank you?

If you just say thank you without quantifying it, you could be giving all sorts of unwanted messages. Without any detail or any discrimination of who you say thank you to, you might be reinforcing poor performance; in other words, you're saying thank you to that person who came in and did far less than anyone else. In just a second or two, you supported someone to feel OK about operating at lesser quality than you expect. As a result, you will now get more of this.

Equally, even when people have worked well, just saying thank you might not tell them what you would like more of. It's too broad and it's likely to have a different meaning to each individual. Whilst it might make people feel good for a minute or two, it will have less and less meaning the more you say it. Used often it becomes a bland, meaningless phrase which might even end up making people feel frustrated rather than valued.

That's not to say you shouldn't display thanks – of course you should, but at the right time, to the right people and in a detailed way. Say thank you in feedback form – say what you see, at the time you see it, ask a question and make it meaningful and personal, so you get more of what you want. Don't lose the power of thanks by making it a catch-all, even for people whose behaviour doesn't warrant it in that moment; you will be promoting marginal performance at worst and at best you will be offering a bland, nondescript (albeit well-meaning) interaction which will not get you more of the good stuff and less of the bad.

Is All Feedback Good Feedback?

Surely any feedback is better than no feedback? Well perhaps not –
it depends how you give it. It's worth saying that no one intends to
give poor feedback or do it badly, but sometimes we don't stop and
think it through. This means that a well-intentioned thank you or
motivational interaction suddenly becomes something damaging.

I came across a good example of this when I was working with a group
of managers on appraisal techniques. It's worth acknowledging
that if you have great Coaching for Leadership skills, you will
automatically have great appraisal skills – because the skills are the
same! In our group, we were discussing our previous experiences of
appraisals throughout our careers, in order to set some context for
our ongoing learning. One manager offered a very useful example
of how good feedback intentions go bad.

This experienced facilities manager described a previous role and
the appraisal he had there with his line manager. The appraisal
was well planned, in advance and with time to prepare. The
meeting went well, and the line manager had worked hard to
prepare her feedback. She offered the facilities manager some
good, detailed feedback about his performance with examples to
illustrate what she was pleased with. The negative feedback was
minimal and constructive, and they discussed how improvement
and development might occur. In all, the facilities manager felt
it had so far been one of the best appraisal meetings of his career.
He was clear about what was going well, what wasn't so good and
how this might be rectified. He reported a sense of motivation and
commitment as a result and felt a strong, loyal working relationship
with his boss.

However, on his way out of the room at the end of the appraisal
meeting, his boss said one short sentence which destroyed all the
good work done in that meeting. She said, "Of course, you've still

a long way to go before you'll be as good as the person in the role before you."

When he was describing his experience, the facilities manager explained that whilst he knew the meeting itself had been a good one, the act of being compared to his predecessor in a detrimental way caused lasting damage. He suddenly felt insignificant and as if all his hard work counted for nothing. He also felt that his line manager was paying lip service to his good work rather than valuing it authentically. The result was a very poor experience, even though to that point the meeting had been a very positive event.

This example reflects that whilst leaders may be highly skilled at offering feedback that is constructive and developmental, one slip-up can cause potentially irrevocable damage. With the benefit of a few years of hindsight and reflection, the facilities manager had developed the experience and wisdom to look back on the incident with some humour. He was able to realise that his line manager hadn't intended to wipe out all the good work achieved in the appraisal meeting, neither had she intended to cause difficulties or demotivate him. However, the sadness is that she did indeed do all those things for the duration of their work together. This means that she never achieved the best from him – either in his capacity to achieve excellence in his role or in her relationship with him.

Giving feedback badly is just as detrimental as giving no feedback at all. It is particularly destructive when we compare one team member with another. Of course, comparisons have to be made – we need to benchmark and be sure that we measure performance and outcomes against tangible markers. However, other people are not tangible markers. When we compare people with each other, it becomes personal and open to bias. We inevitably form different kinds of relationships with each member of our team, which leaves us open to subjective favouritism, no matter how objective we strive to be. Therefore, our feedback needs to be benchmarked against objective markers – our company standards, policies and job descriptions.

Keeping it Relevant

If we are tired or highly stressed, we are much more likely to notice the negative performance in others. This makes it harder to notice good performance and comment on it constructively. The danger is that if we're not self-aware at these times, our feedback can fall into the 'damaging' category very easily.

I recall an incident with a former line manager from some years ago; it was a small issue but because of the way the feedback was delivered, I recall it well. I particularly recall how it made me feel and how tempted I was to withdraw completely as a result.

It had been a particularly busy time in the team and there was a great deal of work on. I had been working long hours and I felt that we had achieved a great deal in terms of outcomes for the business, despite this. I was proud of my team and whilst I couldn't claim perfection, I felt their performance warranted praise and recognition.

My line manager became highly critical when she was tired and stressed and had a tendency to focus on small, negative details, which became the sole focus of her feedback. In amongst all the busy-ness and hard graft, she pulled me to one side and launched into a tirade of criticism. Despite all the positive work and teamwork, her singular piece of feedback was a rant about a spelling mistake on an agenda for a forthcoming workshop meeting.

Whilst I am the first to acknowledge that quality and attention to detail are essential, at that moment in our work this feedback was wholly irrelevant. Her outburst firstly highlights why awareness and calmness are essential in the delivery of good feedback;

secondly, why careful thought is so necessary when ensuring that performance is highlighted in a meaningful way. Using feedback to manage performance is about getting more of the good and less of the bad. The team were delivering well on objectives, yet her feedback was centred entirely on the negative – a very small negative in comparison to the work going on.

I recall the feelings I had in response. I felt angry, protective of my team, and resentful that all the positive achievements were disregarded in favour of a seemingly irrelevant negative detail. This was wholly unhelpful to our ongoing work and our relationship. In fact, my response to her was, "Well if that's all you've got to complain about with everything that's going on now, I feel pretty happy with my work!"

This was not the outcome she expected and equally was not an interaction with my boss that I look back on with pride. It was destructive and did not create a constructive way forward for either of us. It did nothing to improve performance or ensure quality work. Timing, awareness, calmness and meaningfulness are all crucial elements in relevant feedback for performance.

A Lack of Questions and Follow-through

Giving great feedback, as a day to day leadership activity, is the first element in ensuring we avoid marginal and poor performance in our teams. It is also the first step in tackling performance issues. However, even if we do get this aspect right, it isn't a guarantee of success. Although we've discussed it previously in this book, it's worth highlighting again: your leadership becomes more powerful when you follow feedback with questions and then you make sure you follow through on the agreed outcomes.

It's again worth considering what happens in the absence of questions and follow-through in managing performance. Let's suppose you are working to improve the performance of a team member who can't be judged as terrible but you know this person is capable, and perhaps more importantly, is being paid to perform better. You begin giving feedback, consistently and calmly, based on the behaviours you see; relevant and meaningful in the moment you see it. So far, so good. But imagine the scenario if it stops there. You give some great feedback but then your team member never hears about it from you again. There's no conversation around the feedback and you don't bring it to their attention again. What message does this 'one-off' approach to feedback give?

If you're lucky, it'll hit the mark, the performance will improve, and you'll never have to mention it again. More likely though, this behaviour is ingrained because no one has ever mentioned it before. When behaviours have become 'normal' to the individual, that is, when they have been repeated by that person over and over, a one-off piece of feedback is very unlikely to have any impact at all.

Likely, you will feel frustrated because nothing has changed. Your team member will feel puzzled at best. They might walk away from your feedback conversation mulling over their own questions: "Why is my manager mentioning this to me?" "What's changed, I always do it like this?" "Why am I being targeted, I've done it like this for the whole time I've worked here?" At worst, these kinds of questions can create tensions and conflict if left to fester. A little more input is needed to ensure you tackle performance issues with compassion, respect and like you care about what happens next.

Factors Affecting Performance

Before we revisit the techniques of questioning and follow-through in this context, it's worth considering what affects people's performance at work. In other words, what aspects of our lives make the difference between working well and working poorly?

Before you read on, just take a few moments to consider what might be causing those members of your team to function less well than you would like.

When I raise this question with groups of managers, I mostly get some superficial 'off the cuff' responses first. These usually include: 'they don't care'; 'they're lazy'; 'they don't have a very strong work ethic'; 'they're just trying to cause trouble'. I'm sure you came up with a few more of your own.

What's interesting is that there is no research to back up that any of these issues are the main causes of poor and marginal performance in the workplace. There are four main areas which affect performance and by far the most prolific is that of *ability*. As leaders, we assume that every one of our team is equipped to do their job well. After all, they've had the induction, the mandatory training and they've worked on the job for enough time to know what to do.

But what if they haven't? How do you know? When did you check on the calibre of training and mentoring that was given in the first instance? Can you, with absolute certainty, say that this person was properly trained and supported and is entirely clear about the job, the standards and the expectations of their performance? If your answer is yes, ask yourself again, how do I know? Because if you can't evidence it, you may have to accept that it might not be the case. In most cases of poor performance, ability is the culprit and leaders compound it because they assume that everyone got what they needed from the start.

The good news is that of the four factors which most affect work performance, this is the easiest to rectify. The difficult bit is to face the frustration and disappointment of the individual when they realise they haven't been performing well but no one bothered to mention it to them. You can get over this by leading with love;

caring, authenticity and a genuine regard for what happens next is by far the most human way to move on.

After that, after you've given a great piece of feedback about the performance, there are questions to be asked:

"What would help you best to improve on this?"

"How can I help you?"

"What learning/training might you need?"

"What support would you like and who might give you this?"

All you have to do is listen and then act on what you hear. This is not about your solutions or your opinions about what is needed. If you want engagement and a real shot at improving performance, act to switch on your colleague's brain and support them to solve this problem in the best way for them.

Belief is the second factor which affects work performance. Whether confident and self-assured, or timid and insecure at work, these attitudes will be based on beliefs about ourselves. Too much in either direction can create problems of performance. Unfortunately, beliefs are extremely difficult to change; they are ideas and values that we hold about ourselves which are rooted very deeply in our psyche and which have usually been embedded there for a long time.

Whilst we all have doubts from time to time, or experience that flash of 'imposter syndrome', deeply held beliefs about ourselves can have a profound impact on how we carry out our roles. If you hear people say things like "I'm only a (insert job role here)" or "I'm not very good at (insert a long list of tasks here)" or "I didn't do well at school/I can't learn anything/I'm rubbish at…" then you'll know you have belief issues on your hands.

Often people perform poorly because they don't believe they're good enough to do anything else. If you want to be a leader who loves, you need to listen for belief obstacles to good performance. You really do need to care whether this person believes they can do a good job; if they don't believe it, it'll be a self-fulfilling prophecy.

If you suspect beliefs are hindering good performance, your questions might be:

"What makes you think that?"

"How do you know?"

"Where is the evidence of that?"

"How might it be different?"

"What would you need to do to get better at it?"

"What are you good at?"

"How could you use your other skills to be better at this?"

With questions like these, you may begin to get your team members to start to think differently about themselves and, better still, to start questioning their beliefs. Looking for evidence to see if they are 'true' is a good way for some people to start to think differently. However, if deep-rooted beliefs are hindering work performance, I would encourage you to seek the input of a trained coach to help with the complex task of unpicking what is holding this person back from greatness.

Motivation is the third factor affecting performance. This is a huge topic and we will only make a brief mention of it here – there is plenty more information to inform you in the literature and online. Motivation can make an enormous difference to the standard of work and it creates poor and marginal performance if it's lacking.

Generally speaking there are two types of motivation: intrinsic and extrinsic. Put simply, this means that we might be motivated by internal states such as achievement, aspiration and ambition; or external states such as status, money and recognition. Neither is good or bad, better or worse and we all experience some of each. Equally, we are all different – each member of your team will be motivated by different things. If you want to ensure motivation is high and is impacting performance, you need to learn what motivates each one of them.

To do this you have to genuinely care about people and respect the things they are motivated by, whether they are familiar to you or not. Attentive listening gives you the means to do this. Care enough to really hear what's going on for each individual and what drives them. The questions you might ask are:

"What stops you from doing...?"

"What excites you about coming to work?"

"What makes you determined/ambitious?"

"What makes you feel like you want to do a great job?"

"Why do you stay working here?"

"What makes you feel like you don't want to stay here?"

A word of warning regarding motivation. The jury is out as to whether one person can motivate another; what is agreed is that it is possible for one person to demotivate another. If you have a demotivated team, look at yourself first. Some of the most difficult teams that I've ever worked with are those who are being demotivated by their manager. Your team will be a mirror of you; if you are enthusiastic and motivated, your team are much more likely to be. If you lead like you care, then your team are much more likely to care too.

Finally, *external factors* are the fourth issue to consider when working with poor and marginal performance. Your attention might stray here if you have a team member who has previously done great work, but for some reason has had a dip in performance. If you know someone can do the job well – because you've seen them do it – and then suddenly they don't, it may be because something significant is happening in their life.

Some managers believe that personal lives are to be left outside of work. I would urge you to think differently. By picking up a book with 'love' in the title, I'm going to assume that you're pretty in tune with concepts of holism and person-centredness. I would urge you though to seek evidence that you 'live' this: do you genuinely love your colleagues enough to care what happens to them? Are you sufficiently knowledgeable about human behaviour to know that what you invest you get back? If you invest nothing in your people, it's unsurprising when that's exactly what you get back.

I'm not suggesting you turn into a counsellor or professional friend to your people – we covered those pitfalls earlier. I just ask that you care. Your questions might be:

"What do you need?"

"How can I help?"

"Who might help you best with this?"

Follow the questions with a healthy dose of attentive listening and then act on what you hear. Make this about them, not you. Invest in helping your team member to overcome their issue and the by-product will be a faster return to great performance. Along the way, you will likely enhance positive working relationships, loyalty and commitment.

What Exactly is Good Performance?

Another consideration of course is how do you know what good performance is? If you don't know what good looks like, how do you measure when it's not good and how bad it really is? When offering feedback on performance it's essential that you comment not only on the behaviour but ensure its relevance to tangible performance standards.

So how do you know what good looks like? Again, I've asked this question of many managers throughout my research. When we discuss it, their realisation is normally that they're measuring performance on very subjective processes. They say things like, "I just know" or "You can tell when someone is good – they go the extra mile." Some managers even measure good performance on whether someone does what they're told without question! But when we try to break it down, they can't say with certainty what the criteria for good are.

Initially when we try, they may say things like, "Good is when people do what they are supposed to/when they follow their job description." Is this true? Is that good or is that merely satisfactory? Do you rate someone as performing well if they turn up on time? If they get to the end of the day without making a mistake? If they manage to achieve everything they were supposed to? Surely these are all the things you pay them for, so can you rate this good performance or simply meeting the basic expectation?

Setting clear, certain performance expectations is the first, most crucial aspect of achieving great performance and managing poor performance in your teams. Setting out what you expect and checking that everyone understands this is crucial in judging how people are performing. Not having clear expectations which everyone understands is like setting out on a journey without having a destination in mind. The likelihood that you'll wander round aimlessly is very high and this is analogous to what will happen in the workplace if you don't.

You don't need to reinvent the wheel for this; your expectations already appear objectively in the form of job descriptions and requirements and your company policies and procedures. You may also have guidelines and codes of conduct specific to your work sector. All you have to do is make sure you use them as your measure of satisfactory performance. You might just be glad if everyone achieves 'satisfactory': the job gets done with the appropriate responsibility and accountability from everyone. Coaching for Leadership techniques will help you to get there and once you have, you can move on to articulate what 'good' looks like. Keep up with Give the Feedback, Ask the Question and robust follow-through and you have the recipe for a high-performing team.

The Importance of Follow-through

The final piece of the puzzle is follow-through. We have explored this in detail in earlier chapters and now need to place it in the context of performance management. You have given some great behaviour-based feedback, you have asked questions relevant and meaningful to the situation, and you have shown that you give a damn about the person and what happens next. Their brain is in the 'on' position but your work is not yet complete.

You must now ensure you embed the changes, particularly if the individual has been working at 'marginal' level for some time. The brain needs time and support to make and sustain the thinking required for performance improvement, and your follow-through will make or break the success of this. If you never mention it again, things will inevitably return to how they were before, so ensure you keep the situation 'live' through respectful, caring conversations:

- Start with great feedback and have a question-based conversation to establish understanding and suggestions of how things will improve

- Ensure the improvement actions come from your team member, not you, to ensure engagement and optimum motivation

- Establish timeframes and success measures – ask your team member to identify when they will make changes by and how they will know changes are successful

- Make a note of the timeframe and then catch up with your team member at that time

- Ask how they feel things are improving and offer some observations of your own on progress

- Ask questions which help your team member to identify next steps and actions, or if improvement has been achieved then thoughts on how they will sustain this

- Set further follow-up dates to give and receive feedback and update action plans, until the improvements are embedded and consistent

- Do not stop revisiting until you are both confident that improvements can be sustained into the long term

Whilst these steps may seem onerous, in practice they are simple and fast.

Imagine a scenario where a team member has consistently fallen below expectations. Since you have been their line manager they have produced 10% less business than the company average and 15% less than the baseline expectation. They seem oblivious to this and also to the fact that their colleagues don't want to work with them, believing they are lazy and indolent. You plan to tackle the performance issue using Coaching for Leadership techniques:

> Leader: "I notice from the reports this year that you have achieved 10% less business than our company average. Your performance is 15% lower than our company expectation of you."

> Colleague: "Really? I thought everything was fine – no one has mentioned this to me before, so why are you telling me now?"

> Leader: "You didn't know this? What expectations were agreed with you when you first came into post?"

> Colleague: "None – I was thrown in the deep end and just got on with it. No one mentioned anything, so I thought I was doing fine."

> Leader: "I'm sorry that was the case, I hadn't realised that you weren't given the usual training and support. We have an opportunity to move things forward now. What do you need to help you do that?"

> Colleague: "Well it would be helpful to see the reports and work through them to understand what's going wrong and how I can pick it up."

> Leader: "Let's meet tomorrow and I'll have the reports ready for us to work through together."

Tomorrow:

> Leader: "Here are the reports – how can I help you understand them better?"

Colleague: "Give me some time and I'll come back to you."

Leader: "How much time do you need?"

Colleague: "I'll need until tomorrow."

Leader: "OK, let's meet at 2pm tomorrow to discuss your thoughts."

The next day:

Leader: "I noticed you didn't come to our meeting at 2pm, so I came to find out what you've taken from the reports."

Colleague: "Oh, yes it slipped my mind. I can see where I've been missing the targets and I think if I rearrange my schedule I can make up the deficit."

Leader: "OK, when do you think you can achieve that by?"

Colleague: "I think you'll see a difference in my figures by this time next week."

Leader: "OK, let's follow up again then. Who might be able to help you with this?"

Colleague: "I think my assistant could help with rescheduling my diary commitments. I'll ask her this afternoon."

Leader: "Let's meet again this time next week to see how you are doing. I'll make the up-to-date reports available so we can see how things are going."

The next week:

Colleague: "I've come to give you some feedback on my progress. My calculations suggest that I'm now meeting targets as required."

Leader: "Yes, my reports say the same, well done. Is there anything else you need to make sure you can keep up with the additional work?"

Colleague: "No, I'm pretty confident that I know where the problem is and how to deal with it now, thank you."

Leader: "OK, let's review in a month to make sure all is well."

Of course, this example is bland and contrived – you will have a relationship with your people, and conversation and ongoing dialogue will bring the situation to life. All you have to do is genuinely care – both for your colleagues and for the business. Creating optimum performance in people is essential in creating peak business success. Ensuring your team perform satisfactorily to the business expectation and optimally to a high standard is the measure of great leaders. Coaching for Leadership techniques create the mechanism for achieving performance easily, efficiently and with elegantly powerful outcomes.

CHAPTER ELEVEN

Using Coaching for Leadership to Manage Conflict

Conflict is an area we all avoid, particularly at work where the 'fallout' can impact on morale, relationships and the bottom line. Most human beings 'don't do conflict' because it feels uncomfortable and our inner voices warn us that we might not be liked or respected or be able to maintain our relationships if we engage with conflict head on. Whilst intellectually we understand that conflict is normal, even healthy, in practice we rarely look at it positively or constructively. Avoidance is the key, often at all costs, but what if you could feel confident enough to deal with conflict knowing that you have the skills to manage it well, ensure outcomes are positive and enable people and the team to move on easily from it? Even better, what if you could generate ideas and innovation from the conflict within your teams?

By now it won't surprise you to learn that Coaching for Leadership skills are transferable to many situations, conflict included. This chapter will help you place your skills to ensure you approach and manage conflict in the workplace with positive outcomes. Of course, the collaborative approach isn't a 'one size fits all' tactic and occasionally it won't work – particularly in those situations where people dig in and refuse to budge towards a compromise. We'll look at a technique for mediation, for those rare occasions when Coaching for Leadership doesn't work.

What is Conflict?

We normally describe conflict as a negative interaction between one or more people, which has the potential to create antagonism, arguments and lack of cooperation between team members. Leaders I have worked with say they spend unacceptable amounts of work time dealing with petty squabbles and workplace clashes between teammates. Others describe how horrendous it is to manage the daily load when there is all out war between colleagues who refuse to negotiate or compromise towards a solution, so everyone can get back to their work.

Conflict generates ill-feeling; it creates factions in teams when people take sides; individuals moralise and gossip and there will always be someone who fuels the drama and maintains the problem far longer than necessary. These are all the reasons we avoid facing it at all costs – the consequences of doing it badly are far-reaching. A disruptive and unpleasant environment is sufficient for us to do whatever it takes to cover it over and pretend it isn't there.

Intellectually at least, we do of course realise that conflict can also be positive. As leaders, we can discuss the value that conflict brings:

it generates creativity, brings new ideas, prevents teams from becoming stuck and unimaginative, and promotes inventiveness.

Conflict can happen interpersonally, intra- or inter-groups in the workplace. In other words, antagonism can occur between two individuals, more individuals within a team or within teams themselves. There is of course the conflict that happens internally to us personally when we are faced with individual struggles that require input to resolve. Self-coaching techniques are extremely helpful in resolving internal conflict, but this is a lengthier topic for a forthcoming book.

Without doubt, the most difficult aspect of conflict, however it happens, is to tolerate the discomfort it creates. We have already touched on how beneficial a mild discomfort can be in generating thinking and turning that thinking into action. As a reminder, neuroscience evidence suggests that in order for the brain to tip over from contemplating to acting, there must be an element of mild discomfort. Coaching techniques can help to create discomfort, through generating a second or two of silence and also from asking elegant questions. However, in conflict situations the problem is reducing extreme discomfort to a sufficiently mild version for constructive and rational thought to take place.

When Conflict is Destructive

Coaching is far less likely to be successful if there is high emotion attached to the situation. Negative emotions cause extreme discomfort and where this occurs, the conflict is at its most destructive. Antagonistic behaviours tend to escalate, and the experience of the conflict grows disproportionately to the original situation. The key to Coaching for Leadership in conflict situations is to reduce the emotions to a milder level, where constructive dialogue and rational thinking can take place.

The first place where emotions must be brought under control is in yourself as leader. If emotions are running high in you personally, the likelihood that you'll give great feedback or ask relevant questions is significantly lowered. Acknowledgement and recognition of the emotion you are feeling is crucial. If the conflict is between you and someone else, you may be feeling frustrated, offended, distressed or even intimidated. If the conflict is between others in your team, it is likely you'll feel disappointed, angry or irritated by the intrusion into your service. Whatever the emotion, it needs to be controlled in order to deal with the conflict quickly and efficiently.

Once you're aware of your emotion, name it and then deal with it. Don't try to eradicate it completely – that isn't realistic and we all come with messy emotions attached. Emotions are part of caring and people need to see that you actually do give a damn about this. But you must be in control. Remember that high emotion brings a loss of rational thinking.

I can't tell you how to do this. The way we de-escalate or relax down is individual to each of us. Do whatever you do to calm and clear your head. You know yourself best and you know how you normally find peace and composure. Go ahead and do whatever it is before you look to tackle the conflict.

Equally, each member of your team will calm differently too. They may not be as proficient as you in identifying emotion or dealing with it, so you may have to help here. If you're ready (sufficiently calm enough) to tackle the conflict, notice where others are in the emotions stakes. If feelings are running high, do something to de-escalate them. Suggest time out, a walk, a break, or whatever is needed to reduce the passion attached to the issue. Don't engage with Coaching for Leadership techniques unless this is achieved, or you won't stand a good chance of creating a successful outcome.

Dealing with Conflict

Before you wade into a conflict situation, ask yourself who is the best person to deal with this. As a manager, if our team is in conflict and it's affecting the work, our automatic position is that of we should be dealing with it. But is this entirely helpful? The work community is no different from the community at large. Here are a group of people in reasonably close proximity, existing together. Generally, people find harmonious ways of being together, sometimes they can't. Beliefs, opinions and desires conflict and problems occur – this is normal life. Compare how you might expect an adult in the community generally to deal with conflict against how you expect conflict to be dealt with in the workplace.

Out in the world we likely anticipate that an average adult will find themselves in conflict with others from time to time. They'll either deal with it or avoid it and life goes on. If they don't deal with it well, it might escalate, but time passes and the conflict dissipates at some point. At work, it's a little more difficult; it's not OK to avoid it because if it isn't already, it might end up affecting the quality of work or work outputs. It's also risky to deal with it badly because it will almost certainly impact negatively on business.

What is interesting is that unless something illegal occurs, we almost always expect an adult in the world at large to deal with their own conflicts themselves. At work, everyone automatically assumes it's the job of the manager to deal with it. This is an anomaly that reinforces parent-child relationships and gets in the way of accountable, adult behaviours. The key is to maintain adult-adult relationships and accountable and responsible behaviours at all times.

So, the first question to ask yourself is how far do you need to get involved? If you assume you need to deal with it, you may be 'taking on the monkey' and preventing your team from doing their own problem solving. These are adults and you would expect them to deal with their own conflicts outside of work, so why not in it? When I posed this question to groups of leaders, they all agreed. Many realised that they had been using their own valuable time to sort the troubles of people who were perfectly capable of sorting them out for themselves. A further measure that parental styles of leadership were the norm was the realisation that team members were approaching leaders and asking them to deal with it rather than dealing with it themselves. If you wouldn't expect your team members to be calling their parents to help out with conflicts in their out of work life, why would you expect a manager to deal with them inside of work?

I'm not suggesting you never need to get involved. Inevitably you will from time to time, but don't make this the norm or expectation. Equip your team to deal in adult ways with the troubles they encounter; they already know that managing conflict is part of everyday life, they just don't necessarily know that it's a reasonable expectation to do it at work as well.

From a Coaching for Leadership viewpoint, it simply looks like this:

> Leader: "I've noticed that there is some tension between the two of you. I'm concerned that it's affecting your work and interrupting the work of the rest of the team." (feedback)

> Leave a second of silence. If they begin a 'he said/she said' or blame conversation, give further feedback:

> "At this stage, I'd prefer not to get involved with the detail. I trust you to sort this out between yourselves, so we can all get back to work."

Then ask the question:

"How are you going to sort this out?"

Stop talking and let thinking happen. Stop any attempts to give details or blame each other – repeat your statement from before. If further thinking time is needed, offer this and suggest a time when your colleagues will report back on how they have decided to move forward.

Don't feel negatively if things aren't as smooth as you'd like. People will need time to adapt to the change in style and expectation, particularly if they are used to you wading in to sort their problems for them. The essential aspects are to ensure emotions and discomfort remain at a low enough level for rational thinking and dialogue; that you keep a step removed from the detail and avoid taking over the problems of your team; and you maintain your observation of the situation, either to confirm that it is now sorted, or so you are ready to step in should the situation escalate.

How Much Do You Even Need to Know?

In discussions with many leaders, I have asked their opinions on what they need to get involved with. In other words, how much do you need to know about what conflicts there are within your teams? For example, we discussed a scenario where the manager overhears two team members arguing loudly in a public area of the business. Most leaders reply that this is unacceptable and they would intervene immediately as a result. This is a sound observation of course – public conflict is uncomfortable for customers and bad for business.

They go on to explain what they would do next. Most say that they would take the arguing colleagues to a private place and ask what is going on. They want to find out what happened and what is involved. I would urge caution here however. The moment you start digging for the detail, you are now involved. Your time, your resource and your potential to become the parent in the situation are all at risk. Ask yourself, when the conflict is at this stage, do you really need to get involved?

A quick Give the Feedback, Ask the Question intervention may be all you need to manage the conflict:

In the private space, you say "I notice that you were arguing loudly in a public area. Customers could overhear you and this is unacceptable."

You create one second of silence, followed by a question:

"How are you going to sort this out?"

Then you stay quiet and allow your team members to think about their actions and their solutions. Don't get bogged down by detail – you need solutions and outcomes, nothing more. If they aren't forthcoming or emotions seem to be escalating, send them away to calm and think and meet up again later. Expect them to give you solutions, not the other way around. Be clear that you expect adult, accountable behaviours by charging them to deal with it professionally without your intervention.

In reality, you don't need to know the ins and outs of everyone's issues. In fact, it's often better not to know – this way you can stay out of the time-consuming detail and ensure professional outcomes in a fraction of the time. You become less parental and reflect support for appropriate behaviour and return to acceptable working practices.

Parenting and Rescuing

Often, we attempt to avoid the discomfort of conflict by shielding our teams from anything that might cause it in the first place. We encourage our colleagues to report everything to us and equally we may discourage others from approaching our teams with feedback. Whilst at first glance this may appear a supportive stance, it in fact disables people from behaving like the responsible, intelligent adults they are. We all need to learn to give and receive feedback, negotiate, compromise and work with others to reach solutions and promote development. Staying out of conflict and allowing colleagues to function independently with others, at least in the first instance, enables accountability and reduces leadership time spent on conflict.

An example of this is a recent encounter I had with a middle manager in finance. He was in his mid-thirties and managed a team of four or five people. We were discussing Coaching for Leadership skills and he was describing how he managed feedback from other teams to his own. His team were responsible for undertaking work which impacted on the ability of other teams to do their work. Inevitably, feedback came at times from the managers of other such teams, both good and bad. The manager was adamant that when there was negative feedback to be given by another team's manager, this was to come to him, not to the team member themselves.

He felt this was appropriate because he wanted to be a supportive leader. He also wanted to vet any feedback in case it was going to be upsetting for anyone. He wanted to be able to decide what his team members heard and how it was delivered. He was very certain that he should be the one to decide what his team could or should hear and that if it was negative, he should deliver it.

Through questions, he responded that if the feedback was positive or if someone had praise for his team members, then he felt comfortable that it could be delivered directly to them. He seemed completely unable to see that his behaviour was parental and gave the impression that his team needed shielding or rescuing from others. In other words, they aren't capable of receiving, discerning or learning from others' observations of performance. He felt he was 'helping' his team, when in fact others in the group could see that he was potentially disabling them.

To help him view the situation differently, I asked him why he felt it was OK for them to receive positive comments from others but not those which were adverse. He said that they were young and he didn't want anyone to upset them. He felt able to take the feedback and translate it into something more palatable for them. With further dialogue however, it transpired that all of his team members were in their early thirties – only a couple of years younger than him.

We started to shift his thinking somewhat when we began to make comparisons with their life outside of work. The manager lived independently with his partner and family as did the rest of his team. I asked him who helps them with difficulties and difficult conversations when they aren't at work. Somewhat surprised, he seemed lost for an answer, so I asked him more specifically whether a parent was likely to be called on by his team members when they encountered negative conversations or incidences at home. It was only when he was able to recognise the independence and abilities of his colleagues outside of work that he realised his 'help' was creating a team of dependent people at work, who were losing valuable skills of discourse and personal development.

Our colleagues don't need managers who rescue them. They need leaders who respect their abilities and encourage them to develop; who value independence in teams and grow this to ensure problem solving occurs naturally and creatively. This includes supporting them to dig deep and manage their own conflicts in the knowledge that at times this may escalate to a point where leadership intervention is required. At these times, you will be confident and knowledgeable to intervene in the most effective way, using Coaching for Leadership skills.

Helping and Supporting

Through the journey of learning and using Coaching for Leadership skills, leaders often need to redefine their thinking about what supporting and helping their teams actually means. We have already discussed how directive styles of leadership potentially disable people from being the responsible, accountable, competent worker we wish for; that said, when we are directive it really is only from a desire to help and support. This is what we think we are doing when we wade in, protect and rescue, give people answers to problems and freely give of our opinions and experience before we've even found out properly what's going on.

Help and support from this moment forward comes from a place of enablement. Helping means facilitating our teams to seek the outcomes and answers that are right for them. Supporting means offering feedback so that people know what is needed and what isn't, and from asking questions to help them decide how they might achieve this.

Often when managers are first learning to use collaborative and facilitative styles of leadership, they say they feel like they aren't helping their teams anymore. Some even say that their teams accuse them of being unhelpful or unsupportive because they're not readily telling them what to do any longer. This transition takes time and practice for the leader and their teams. Everyone needs time to consider the changes and appreciate that when whole teams transition to collaborative adult working, job satisfaction improves because independence and accountability are valued.

When conflict occurs, people don't need a parent in the workplace. They need help to see that conflict is bad for morale and business and that everyone will be expected to deal professionally with conflict when they experience it. They need support to see it through; to realise that they are trusted to come up with ways of making it work; that they are accountable to the leader and the rest of their team to ensure this doesn't impact performance. They will be further helped by observing how their leaders role model behaviours in dealing with conflict themselves.

Using Coaching for Leadership Skills in Managing Conflict

As managers, we find ourselves usually in one of two positions when it comes to conflict. Either we need to deal with conflict between ourselves and someone else, or we need to deal with conflict between two or more of our people.

We have touched on how conflict can be managed between others earlier in this chapter and we will go on to discuss later how conflict can be mediated when initial coaching interventions aren't enough. The leader's life can be a little more difficult to manage when conflict happens between them and someone else, particularly if it's 'up the chain' with their boss. This is because emotion becomes more difficult and we have more invested in dealing with it well. We can often find it more difficult to deal with emotions when they are directed towards us.

I once coached a senior manager who had received a number of complaints about his leadership style. He was described as overbearing, intimidating at times and his team were expressing difficulty in working with him. The fact that he had received these complaints through grievances made to his line manager was particularly difficult and distressing.

The manager thought of himself as a caring and compassionate man and was disturbed that his team felt this way about him. He was highly motivated to manage a successful business with happy staff. Our work began by looking at his style and how this had been shaped through his career.

Still a young man, the manager was sporty and fit. He had always excelled at team sports and had leadership experience as a manager of sports facilities. He was now leading a team in health and social care, a sector close to his heart and future aspirations. Physically, he was very tall and muscular, and he was used to speaking loudly and candidly to everyone around him.

In his new role, the team was unused to this profile of a leader. They quickly misinterpreted his stature and stance as intimidating and his loud and blunt manner of speaking as offensive. Neither leader nor team spent any time considering their different backgrounds and experiences, which led quickly to conflict.

Initially, we worked on ways of reducing the team's sense of intimidation and offence. Through simple things such as sitting down with rather than standing (over much shorter people), he was able to build a level of comfort into his interactions. By working on speaking more quietly and sensitively, he was able to gain trust and respect. None of these practices will be new to seasoned leaders reading this, but it is essential to recollect and remain conscious of methods such as stance, proximity and voice moderation when in conflict situations.

So, if you find yourself in conflict with your boss, your first move will be to sit down. It's much harder to shout and lose control if you're sitting and it's also much harder for them to remain standing if you sit and invite them to do the same. Creating a physical environment which reduces potential high emotion is crucial. Even if it's not your boss who you're conflicting with, these things are so important. Attempting to gain higher status or exude greatest power is never a professional, collaborative way to solve conflict.

In further work with this manager, we established that he always felt 'on the back foot' if someone expressed strong emotion towards him. For example, a member of his team was frequently short-tempered and confrontational towards him, leaving him feeling that he didn't know how to deal with it. His tendency was either to be confrontational in return, which escalated the situation, or he would avoid it altogether. We have already acknowledged in this book that if you allow someone to continue to behave in a particular way, the human brain will default to 'this behaviour is OK because no one has said it isn't' thought. Implicitly condoning poor behaviour is the reason why it continues.

We discussed a Give the Feedback, Ask the Question technique to specifically buy time for the manager to think and find an appropriate way to respond to the confrontational manner of his team member. In a scenario where the manager was approached by his confrontational team member:

> Manager: "You seem to be pretty angry about that this morning…?"

Feeding back the emotion (say what you see, nothing more) is often a good way to broach something difficult. They'll either agree that they are angry, or they'll disagree. If they disagree, you can go on to say:

> "You seem to be feeling something very strongly – what is it you're feeling?"

This opens up the conversation. It also helps the other person to take note of their own strength of emotion. Often people are unaware of this and once they realise, are able to mediate it for themselves. More helpfully, it buys you time to take a breath, get a grip on your own emotions and think about what you want to say next. Your brain will need a fraction of a second only to do this – don't make the mistake of thinking you need hours of thinking time. Trust your brain to do what it's built to do – process very quickly. You'll become even faster with practice.

You can then follow it up with:

> "What do you plan to do about the issue?" or

> "What have you tried so far?" or

> "Who can help you/how can I help you?"

In a very short interaction, you have de-escalated potentially destructive emotion, bought yourself some thinking time and swiftly moved on from unnecessary detail to thinking about solutions, which you have facilitated the team member to take responsibility for himself/herself.

The principle also works well upwards to your line manager. Let's imagine a scenario where your line manager typically calls you late on a Friday afternoon, requesting reports or information. You end up staying late each time to furnish her with what she's requested and it's beginning to cause you frustration and resentment.

Your first action is to consider your stance and to buy yourself some time to get a grip on your emotions and potential responses. Sit down, take a breath and then say what you see (or hear):

> "You'd like me to produce a report on…/find you data on…?"

Stay silent to promote thinking and to buy yourself thinking time. Then:

> "I notice that you've called for information often on a Friday afternoon lately. How urgently do you need the information/

might there be a way I could give you the information sooner/ how might I help to avoid the rush on a Friday afternoon?"

Then stop talking. You will feel slightly anxious if you're not used to questioning your boss. This is normal, but don't allow it to derail your intentions. You need to get what you want without encouraging conflict, so stay quiet. You have now opened up the potential for a respectful, professional and conflict-free conversation. Your boss might not like it, but there is nothing in your manner, tone or conversation that's in any way controversial or unprofessional, so they'll be hard-pressed not to respond in a similar manner.

If your boss is highly emotional, don't be afraid to use similar techniques that we have discussed for your team. Feeding back the emotion is helpful to encourage insight in others. If there is no obvious emotion, but the words someone uses are difficult or antagonistic, simply repeat back verbatim what the person has said. Often when we hear back the words we use, it triggers greater insight and thinking, and we can reflect more deeply on the impact of what we said. All you have to do is repeat back exactly what the person said, without judgment, sarcasm or emotion and then stay quiet. Do the experiment and see how it enhances difficult conversations and manages conflict or potential conflict with the minimum of risk and fuss.

Dealing with Conflict When Coaching for Leadership Doesn't Work

Practising and remaining consistent with the suggested techniques will ensure you diffuse conflicts quickly and confidently and it will minimise the fallout and impact on your business. It will show you really care; you're not ignoring conflict and you're not getting caught up in it, but you are clear about what you expect adults to do in your workplace. You care about accountability and competence and you're prepared to work to get it in your team. That said, with the best will in the world, a conflict will occasionally spill over to a level where you have no choice but to intervene.

If things become serious and there seems no chance that the conflict will be solved without you, a mediation technique may be the answer to sorting it out and moving on. All of the above principles still stand; you'll have tried them already and the techniques are still embedded in the mediation process you move on to.

There are many principles and processes for managing conflict in the literature and online. You can easily equip yourself with contemporary thinking in this field and there are many mediation techniques to choose from. I have chosen a simple, five-step process which is easily implemented and should move you to a resolution swiftly. The process remains collaborative rather than directive and you will facilitate your conflicted team members to reach the solutions most appropriate to them.

Stage 1 – Agree the ground rules, set the scene

This first stage is critical to the success of the mediation meeting. You'll create an environment which is private, uninterrupted and sets the scene for a serious and professional meeting to take place. This is not about intimidating scene-setting, but neither is it about a coffee and a chat. This conflict has become sufficiently serious for you to intervene, so its resolution needs to be robust and have gravitas. Make sure that everyone involved is aware the meeting is to take place; reassure them it is to bring resolution and closure, not to apportion blame, and give them the chance to reflect and prepare.

At the commencement of the meeting, reiterate that you are not going to go over old ground or lengthy detail. The mission is to find a resolution that is acceptable to all parties. Blame is not apportioned, and the tone of the meeting is a positive one. Your first task is to facilitate those present to agree some ground rules for the work you are about to do.

Ground rules are vital in avoiding messy, emotional meetings which achieve nothing but more angst. It is important that you ask participants to identify what will help them to feel safe and comfortable, to speak honestly and identify positive solutions. You may have to start by suggesting some yourself, to show the way. You should check that all participants feel they can adhere to each ground rule. They should be written down and left somewhere where they can be seen by everyone throughout the course of the conversation.

They may include things like:

- The conversation stays in the room – nothing will be repeated outside of it without the permission of all involved

- Everyone will be courteous and will treat each other with respect

- There will be no shouting or talking over each other

- We will focus on the issues, not people's personalities

- 'I' language will be used – we'll take responsibility for what we say

- We'll express feelings honestly

- We'll respect each other's views, even if they are different from our own

You and your colleagues will come up with these and more as you talk. Plan sufficient time to elicit ground rules thoroughly – it will make all the difference to the professionalism and positivity of your conversation. If anyone breaches the ground rules, calmly remind them of what they agreed and request they adhere to their promises.

Stage 2 – Gather information

This is not a rerun of the whole conflict – you don't need to go back over everything that has happened. Make it clear this is not what you are here for. This stage is about finding out what each party wants as the outcome. Be assertive and don't allow conversation to run into details of failings or insults and character assassinations. Be clear that you would like to hear what each party wishes for, as an end to the conflict. Get detail – be sure that each party has sufficient time and space to clarify exactly what they need for a complete resolution. You will need to use questioning and practise attentive listening to ensure clarity and understanding.

It doesn't matter if each party appears to have different goals. Often there are overlaps and similarities in goals when you dig deep. Look for parallels and connections in what is being said. This stage is simply about identifying the destination, not about deciding how. Avoid straying into the whys and hows of how the goals might be achieved and simply state in detail each person's desires for the resolution of the problem. Whilst this is not about you, you may also want to add your goals for restoring full working order to your team and service.

Stage 3 – Agree the problem

If you take plenty of time with stage 2 and get all the technicolour detail of what each person's goals are, you'll start to have a clear picture of where the discrepancies are. In other words, what the real problem is – the differences in what each person sees as the outcome.

Spend time articulating the problem – try out phrases, words and language that everyone can understand. Get assurances before you move on that you have reached an agreement of what the problem is and looks like now.

Stage 4 – Create possible solutions

Now there is clarity over the problem and the goals, you can move to look at how the goals can be achieved. Everyone must be involved in generating ideas and potential solutions. You can use a brainstorming technique or any other processes you find useful. Some people find it useful to bounce ideas off each other, whereas some prefer a little quiet reflective time to make some notes or write ideas on post-it notes first.

Generate creativity. By now everyone should feel sufficiently safe and relaxed to be creative. Explore options thoroughly and begin to move towards common ground.

Stage 5 – Agree a solution and an action plan

If you're lucky and things are going well, there may be an obvious point of commonality which you can agree easily. However, if it's been trickier, you will need to encourage the parties to accept compromises through negotiation. If this is the case, return to your ground rules as necessary and reinforce the message that this is about resolution to achieve professional outcomes. People don't have to like each other but they do have to work together. Be clear that this is one aspect that is not negotiable.

Any compromise needs to be win-win – a solution which both parties can genuinely agree and adhere to. It is a false win if someone is coerced into accepting something that they cannot or will not abide by once the meeting is over. Take time to assure yourself that the compromise is an honest one, fair to all sides.

Once a compromise has been agreed, set a follow-up date for review. Follow-through is as essential in mediation as it is in Coaching for Leadership or any leadership intervention. You will all have invested time and resources in reaching a resolution, so don't let it slip away. Meet again, or several times if necessary, to ensure everyone is doing what they said they would and the conflict is genuinely resolved. For each meeting, carry the ground rules with you and use them moving forward to create constructive and professional dialogue.

Creative Conflict – Generating Ideas and Innovation

We all need to differ from time to time in order to bring fresh conversations and ideas to the table. My own view is that the ability to debate and argue constructively with each other is a very powerful leadership skill. Of course, we need to be courageous to do this because at times it might involve the risk of someone disagreeing with us, coming up with a better idea or confronting our beliefs about something. However, a crucial role of leadership is to create environments which are innovative and developmental. To not do so risks stale, outdated working practices, losing business and good people.

If you are proficient at collaborative and facilitative leadership and you practise Coaching for Leadership and Give the Feedback, Ask the Question, you will already have a solid platform for creative and innovative working. This is because you have already switched on the thinking capacity of your teams; you have also demonstrated that you expect and trust your teams to be adult, accountable and to solve their own problems.

You can move this forward and create conflict – in a positive sense, for ideas and innovation – with a couple of simple techniques. You may already have mechanisms by which people can make suggestions about their workplace or perhaps nominating team members for recognition. Make full use of these by paying attention and listening attentively to the messages your colleagues are giving. Don't dismiss things out of hand without thorough contemplation – sometimes the most creative ideas come from the most eccentric thoughts. Reward colleagues for ideas and creativity rather than longevity in the job. Do things which show you value positive conflict and the creativity generated by it.

You might also try giving your staff meetings a make-over. I often challenge leaders to replace their normal meeting agendas with questions instead of information. In other words, to replace the types of meeting where the chairperson does all the talking, usually information giving, with something different. What might it look like to your team if you asked the questions and they did the talking? What might you gain from inviting positive conflict – encouraging professional and positive debate and celebrating the ideas and innovation generated by it? Be sure to set your ground rules at the start and sit back and enjoy the difference your new-look meetings bring.

Conflict creates a great many headaches for leaders and requires more time and resources than most leaders have to resolve. Whilst it is tempting to avoid conflict, cover it over or become embroiled in it, it is worth working on a few simple skills to manage it well. Confidence and competence ensure that the risk of negative, destructive conflict is minimised or at least dealt with swiftly enough to limit the damage. This leaves leaders with more time and inclination to focus on positive, creative and innovative ways of debating and challenging; of achieving growth and development through embracing and enjoying difference. Through managing conflict like you love your people!

CHAPTER TWELVE

Illustrating the Coaching Style – Case Studies

This final chapter is designed to help you to embed learning and enhance your comprehension through genuine examples. Every example and story here is authentic and has been told by real leaders in actual situations. To preserve confidentiality, the only things that have been omitted are names of people or establishments. Where events might distinguish an individual or organisation, I have taken steps to remove any identifying features.

The anecdotes here have been shared by leaders undertaking the Coaching for Leadership module training, or by leaders who have been involved in my official research. Each has been trained in the techniques described in this book, followed by a period of practice and observation.

Following training, leaders are expected to undertake a period of practice in their normal workplace, with their normal teams. During this time, they are required to experiment with their new learning, utilising the Coaching for Leadership techniques at every opportunity.

Following every Coaching for Leadership interaction or use of techniques, leaders are requested to complete a guided reflection, an example of which is below. You may find it helpful to use reflective practice such as this to embed and strengthen your Coaching for Leadership learning. Use all or part of the following guided reflection to assist you in doing this. All the anecdotes documented in this chapter have been reported using this technique. Leaders are encouraged to return to their learning groups after a period of four to six weeks to share experiences. These stories have been taken directly from the sharing of those experiences.

Reflection Form

Coaching for Leadership

Describe the situation which led up to the coaching episode:

What was your intended outcome of the coaching episode?

What were the questions you asked?

What were the responses and outcomes of those questions?

What went well/not so well?

What are your plans for follow-up with this member of staff?

What would you do differently next time/what different questions might you ask next time?

What learning needs have you identified for yourself?

Date of follow-up and reflections on follow-up outcomes:

Examples of Give the Feedback, Ask the Question

The Team Member Who Wouldn't Train

A general manager responsible for a service with over 100 staff reported some difficulty in motivating her teams to update and refresh required legislative training. Whilst everyone was contracted to ensure regulatory updates in their training, it was an ongoing challenge for the manager to ensure all team members adhered to the requirements. Over time the manager had attempted everything from begging to punishing those who failed to meet their contractual requirements.

There was one team member in particular who was highly resistive to meeting her training obligations. An otherwise exemplary colleague, the manager didn't want to lose her from the service. Nevertheless, an obligation is exactly that. Following her Coaching for Leadership training, the manager decided to attempt to Give the Feedback, Ask the Question to address this long-standing problem.

She called the team member to her office, to create an undisturbed, private space. She then gave the feedback – commenting without judgment or emotion on the behaviour that was the problem:

> "I notice that you still haven't refreshed your fire training, which is now three months out of date."

She created mild discomfort by generating a second or two of silence and then asked the question:

> "Given this is a requirement of your contract to work here, how are you going to ensure you meet your obligations?"

She then stopped talking and calmly waited for a response.

The team member seemed alarmed that she was three months out of date – not seeming to have realised that she was so far behind. She promised that the training would be completed by the end of the week. The manager therefore arranged a further catch-up at the end of the week to follow this through and was delighted when the team member was true to her word.

When reflecting on this outcome, the manager was shocked by how simple it had been to get the job done. She had been telling staff over and over that training had to be done, at meetings, in memos and one-to-one. She realised that 'telling' had switched off the brains of her teams to a point where they just weren't hearing the message anymore. This was further compounded by the fact there was no follow-through; she told staff and then didn't speak to them about it again until the next time she told them.

The manager also realised that the message had been too vague; when she addressed it specifically, with precise data (you are now three months out of date), it suddenly became real and personal for her colleague. When that person was handed the responsibility to sort it and knew the manager would follow-up on it, she went away and did what an adult would do: dealt with it promptly.

The Post-Christmas Tidy-Up

The manager of a 24-hour residential care service described a brief intervention which changed the way her team worked with an ongoing problem. Following the Christmas period, the manager had taken leave for a couple of weeks. When she returned, the festive decorations, additional chairs and paraphernalia were still cluttering a whole room, rendering it unusable for the residents of the service. Not only was it untidy, it also breached regulatory requirements for space and access.

The manager was furious to return from her holidays to find this; she had an experienced team who should have known better. Despite her initial inclination to pull her team in to vent her frustration, she decided to experiment with Give the Feedback, Ask the Question.

She invited her senior team (those who would be responsible for ensuring the tidy-up) into her office to create privacy, although did not invite them to sit down. She wanted it to be a brief, adult-adult interaction, leading to action. She then gave collective feedback:

"I'm just back from holiday in the middle of January and I notice the small lounge is still unusable."

She created silence, during which a couple of the team gave some half-hearted excuses, although she resisted the temptation to respond, continuing the silence to allow thinking in her team.

She then asked the question:

"How has this happened and what are you going to do to rectify it?"

Again, there was a small flurry of comments, which she allowed to be expressed. Then one member of the team said, "Don't worry, we'll sort it." She simply replied, "OK, thank you", they went away and did exactly that. Once the problem was sorted, the manager thanked them for the prompt action and then asked a further question:

"How are we going to make sure this doesn't happen again?"

She didn't wait for an answer however, knowing that the team would continue to think about and process the question if she simply left it with them, so she walked away to ensure her team would reflect on the matter.

When reflecting on the interaction with her learning group, the manager was most surprised at how quickly the matter was dealt with. She acknowledged that normally she would have been angry and frustrated and would probably have spent a few hours tidying up herself – probably exuding anger and frustration but not actually saying anything to anyone. There would have been a lot of emotion – her upset and her team's response to that, of keeping out of her way until things had calmed down again. No one would have discussed the situation and it would have festered away for a while until the next problem occurred.

She could see how much energy it took from her and her team not to deal with issues well. She could also see that with a bit of practice, creating an environment for adult thinking and behaviours was not so difficult. In fact, at the time of the event, she thought she must have got the technique wrong because it was so quick and easy to get a result!

Eating Chips

A very senior director explained a difficulty he regularly encountered when moving around his multisite business. He felt it was important to speak with staff at all levels when he visited sites, but often had difficulty in discussing his negative observations with more junior staff. He realised that his status in the company made this more difficult and on one occasion, even though he attempted to be gentle, he had unwittingly made a member of staff cry. This inhibited his conversations with people and even though instinctively he wanted to be able to discuss things directly with all staff, he found himself avoiding lower ranks, asking managers to pass on messages instead.

One day he visited a site and observed several of the team eating a bowl of chips whilst loitering around the edge of a public customer area. Whilst the organisation provided meals as a perk for staff, the requirement is that they are seated appropriately in the eating area, to maintain the professionalism of the site. Because of past difficulties, he would normally have asked the site manager to intervene. However, he decided on this occasion to try Give the Feedback, Ask the Question.

He approached the group and made his observation:

"I notice you're all standing here eating chips."

The silence he then created was extremely uncomfortable. It was clear no one was going to say anything, and the colleagues were waiting for a reprimand. He understood this was likely due to his status, so he asked a quick question:

"Where should you be having your break?"

The colleagues mumbled apologies and then moved off to an appropriate place to take their break.

Ideally, the director would have preferred more dialogue, although considering the situation he was pleased that a reasonably comfortable and positive interaction had taken place. He felt reassured that he had found a way to have the conversation himself instead of passing it on and recognised this as a positive move towards better staff interactions generally. He wanted to ensure a reputation for being approachable but unafraid to tackle issues, so perceived this as a step towards his goal. He has been using the techniques since and has been pleased with the more positive dialogue he is having with staff at all levels.

Dealing with the Older Manager

An experienced regional manager explained the difficulty he was having dealing with a site manager who was approaching retirement. The site manager was considerably older than him and had worked in the sector for many years. A particular difficulty was that the site manager was extremely reluctant to use technology of any kind. This was causing problems with emails, responses to requests for information and with audits and reports. So far, the site manager had used team members' expertise to complete electronic tasks, but there were a number of actions only she could perform.

The regional manager had much respect for his site manager's age, experience and knowledge and therefore tended either to avoid tackling the issues or else mentioned them in a jokey or light-hearted way. This was not, however, solving the problem and head office were requesting that action be taken.

He decided to use Give the Feedback, Ask the Question as maintaining a positive working relationship with her was extremely important to him. So, his feedback next time he visited her site office was:

> "I notice you seem very reluctant to use the computer for anything."

Following a second of silence he asked:

> "Is this hampering your ability to do everything you need to do?"

To his surprise, she admitted it was and they moved on to have a candid conversation about the difficulties. Give the Feedback, Ask the Question had enabled both to openly acknowledge the 'elephant in the room' and they began to talk about something they had both been avoiding. They were able to take the first steps towards the training and support she needed to gain confidence in using her computer fully. Throughout, the regional manager avoided making suggestions and giving advice. This way he ensured the site manager was respectfully supported to implement actions appropriate for her. The regional manager was able to avoid his fear of patronising or belittling an experienced and esteemed member of his team.

Examples of Using Coaching for Leadership to Manage Performance

That Notoriously Difficult Team Member

During a Coaching for Leadership learning session with a group of senior managers from the same organisation, a conversation began about a team member who everyone seemed to know. Indeed, this team member was notorious for being outspoken, difficult to manage, creating conflicts and refusing to follow instructions. She had worked in most of the teams of the managers present, and each one had moved her on to another team at the earliest opportunity.

The colleague was a likeable, popular and gregarious character, but with a strength and ability to galvanise reactions from her teammates which the managers felt difficult to cope with. She worked hard but only when doing things she liked to do. She created drama, conflict or went off sick when asked to engage in issues she did not choose.

Following the Coaching for Leadership learning, her current line manager felt motivated to attempt a different approach to try to capture her positive traits, to contribute more appropriately to the team. Most importantly, she wanted to achieve a period of stability with the team member where she would fulfil her job role without complaint or issue.

The manager realised that because the team member had behaved this way for many years without serious consequence, she would need to be consistent with a new approach over a period of time. In other words, she was realistic that things would not change overnight and that there would be ups and downs on the way to improved performance from the colleague. She was committed to trying out her new skills in collaborative and facilitative leadership to improve the performance of this notoriously difficult team member.

She began by seeking her out for brief feedback, several times a day. She offered observations of behaviour regularly, good and bad, following up with questions about how to take things forward or ensure problematic behaviours were deterred. Initially, the colleague did not take well to the change. She was mildly sarcastic when offered feedback or shrugged her shoulders when asked a question. The manager remained resolute however, giving the team member the opportunity to go away to think and then following up to ask for a response later on.

After a few days, the manager began to notice a change. She was having more positive conversations with the team member, who was behaving more calmly in the workplace and was generally getting on with her work with less supervision. The manager decided to have a meeting with the team member to discuss her observations.

Over a cup of coffee, the manager gave her colleague feedback about the changes in behaviour she had observed and asked her if she had noticed a difference in herself. The team member said she felt more supported and listened to by the line manager. She said she knew what she was doing well, not just what she was doing wrong, and she liked this. The manager asked her what her career aspirations were and what she would need to feel she was doing a great job.

The team member said she would like to progress and climb the company ladder. She wanted the opportunity to develop and mentor other team members. The manager was surprised when her colleague suggested several ways that the team could approach work differently and decided to support her in making some alterations to working practice.

The manager used questions to ask her colleague what she would change, why and how. Once they had identified two clear projects, with specific actions and goals, she supported her colleague to make the changes. She checked in at regular agreed intervals for progress updates and continued to give daily feedback on her observations, good and bad. After another two weeks, the team member sought out her line manager to tell her that this was the best job she had ever had, and that she was the best manager she had ever had.

Even more surprising to the manager was the ease with which she was able to discuss feedback and challenges with the team member and how responsive and responsible she was in return. The whole team noticed the change and comments were made about how calm and positive the environment had become.

The whole group of managers in the learning session were able to reflect on this Coaching for Leadership example. Most had known the team member in question and none had managed a satisfactory working relationship with her to date. They were able to contemplate the extensive time – totalling hundreds of hours – they had collectively spent on meetings, performance reviews, goal setting and, in some cases, formal action, with this colleague.

Many were incredulous about the transformation. None were complacent that a magical transition would ensue without work – the manager describing her journey with her colleague was well aware that there continued to be hard work ahead, which would require consistent focus and ongoing collaborative leadership effort. However, she felt that the hard work had been worth it; that as hard as it had been, it was far easier than the previous conflicted, emotional dramas; and that whether or not her colleague continued to make a success of her role, she could look herself in the eye and know she had performed to her best leadership skills, to turn the situation around.

Shifting Culture from Induction

Following the Coaching for Leadership learning, a fellow learning and development professional noticed a gap in the induction training he was responsible for. As an employee of a large national company of 10,000 staff, he was responsible for the induction and ongoing training of overseas staff. His company recruited from Eastern Europe and Asia to fill a skills gap, although cultural differences had proved problematic in ensuring these professionals supervised their respective teams to the job role standard. The challenge was how to ensure team leaders from overseas were equipped with the necessary skills and understanding to lead their teams effectively, where differences in language, culture and working practices often hindered smooth functioning.

In the first instance, my L & D colleague built core leadership learning into the initial induction. This served to highlight leadership expectations and responsibilities within the team leader job role. However, it was insufficient to equip the new recruits with the 'how' of the leadership role. Many found that whilst they understood the expectations of the leadership component of their role, language and cultural issues caused a lack of confidence and meant they quickly retreated to the technical aspect of role function, where they were more comfortable. As a result, their teams complained that they had no leadership support, creating unnecessary friction.

My colleague needed a fast way to equip the inductees with simple skills to lead from their first day in the business, which sat outside of language and cultural differences. He experimented with Give the Feedback, Ask the Question as a technique to build leadership confidence. He found that the simplicity of the technique made it easy to learn. People from differing cultural and language backgrounds could comprehend the skills needed and know how to begin to lead others in a collaborative way. It facilitated confidence in them and satisfied teams that both the technical and leadership aspect of roles were being fulfilled.

After induction, all staff with leadership roles were taught Coaching for Leadership skills in depth, as ongoing development. Over time, a culture of collaborative and facilitative leadership developed through the company, with everyone recognising the benefits of adult interaction and attention to developing the business through developing its people.

When Competence Doesn't Match with Position

An interim consultant in a large telecoms company reported an interaction he had with a senior member of the team he was supporting. Initially, he had difficulties even meeting up with this manager; his position as consultant was clearly making her uncomfortable and in a large, multisite organisation, it was easy for her to avoid him.

After a number of weeks, he travelled to see her, expecting a difficult meeting. The previous week, he had experienced a challenging phone call with her, following a review of the team's function. Given the delicate nature of the situation and the need to maintain solid relationships to complete his consultancy objectives, the consultant decided to use Coaching for Leadership skills to ensure collaboration was maximised.

He discovered that the manager had been promoted a little over a year previously, with minimal skills and experience for the role she was now in. She had also received only token support from her line manager. It was clear to the consultant that she had been promoted when her competence did not meet role expectation and she was also suffering from isolation from her manager and the rest of the team.

His main goal became to coach the manager to identify her needs and how she might strengthen both her position and her confidence. Whilst he had many ideas of his own, he realised that the manager herself would need to identify her own problems, and solutions to those problems, to ensure relevance, commitment and sustainability. He therefore refrained from offering his own advice and opinion. Instead he asked questions, listening attentively to the answers before asking more questions.

He reported at the learning session that the meeting, whilst long and focused, was a success. He and the manager worked together on the following issues:

- How to identify and meet her team's priorities

- How to meet compliance requirements and link with others who also have compliance responsibilities

- How to put forward a case for what she needs

- How to say what needs to be said, even when it is difficult

- How to have your voice heard in a team of strong individuals

The consultant reported how drained he felt after the meeting and reflected that asking questions and attentive listening take focused energy to maintain. However, he felt it had been well worth the commitment because of the positive outcomes from the meeting.

His collaborative approach had ensured a productive encounter which remained professional, respectful and supportive.

A few weeks later, the consultant was on a conference call attended by the manager, her line manager and a number of peers from her team. On the call, he heard her using some of the ideas, solutions and techniques she had identified at their meeting to get her point across and achieve outcomes for her team. This offered him the opportunity to measure a degree of success from his Coaching for Leadership interventions. He had actually witnessed the change in her approach first-hand and noted the increased confidence with which she spoke to her manager and peer group.

Examples of Using Coaching for Leadership to Manage Conflict

Is it Forgetfulness or Stealing?

The managing director of a small sales company was having difficulties with an outgoing member of her sales team. Having resigned his position, the team member was concluding required work and paperwork when the MD realised that he still had several hundred pounds worth of demonstration stock in his possession.

The MD had requested the return of the items on a number of occasions, both verbally and by email. On each occasion, the team member had assured her that he would box them up and post them back, apologising for forgetting them the last time.

A self-confessed avoider of conflict, the MD began to feel that she would never get the stock back. The monetary value was less important to her than the ethical behaviour – or her perceived lack of it – from her colleague. Her business was founded on ethical values and her own strong sense of morality was in direct conflict with the behaviour demonstrated by the team member. She wanted to avoid a direct conflict situation with him but could not think of anything more she could do other than threaten legal action.

Following her Coaching for Leadership learning, she decided to put some of the techniques she had learned into practice. She wanted to speak with him directly, but given the great distance between them, this had to be done over the phone. Previously, she had been friendly, mildly apologetic and light-hearted in her conversations with him. This was an attempt to keep things friendly and avoid conflict and ill feeling. She realised that things now had to be different if she wanted to get a different outcome.

She began by giving feedback, which was brief, direct and factual:

> "I notice you still have not returned the stock and this is the fifth time that I've asked you for it."

She then created a second or two of silence, during which she herself became extremely uncomfortable. Not only was she a talker usually but she found herself somewhat anxious that a conflict might ensue. However, she maintained the silence, during which her team member repeated his usual promise of returning the items.

Rather than respond to this, she asked a question instead:

> "Given how many times I've had to ask you, what would you do now if you were me?"

As she recounted her story and reflected on the interaction, she realised what a profound question she had asked. Implicitly, she had asked her team member to decide his own fate. He seemed somewhat taken aback by this and eventually said that he would be tempted to take legal action if he were her.

When others put themselves in your position, they are often harsher with their thinking than you might be. This has the benefit of them identifying their own fate and minimising any conflict or accusations of intimidation. The outcome for the MD was positive. She also had avoided costly, lengthy proceedings which would have been uncomfortable and distracting.

Changing the Action Plan

A team leader used her Coaching for Leadership skills to avoid escalating a conflict between herself and another team leader. She acknowledged that she and her colleague often did not see eye to eye and whilst they managed a professional working relationship, this was fragile.

They almost came to blows when her counterpart altered an action plan for one of her clients, in her absence and without consulting her. On returning from her days off, she discovered that her colleague had made changes to the action plan for one of her key clients. This was an occasional necessity if a client's needs changed drastically in the absence of their allocated key contact, but in this instance the team leader could see no tangible reason why the plan had been changed while she was away.

She recalled how irritated and upset she felt and her instinct was to confront her colleague and demand to know why he had interfered with her client. She was angry and aware that a major conflict could result.

Despite her anger she was keen to avoid a conflict, although it was important for her to understand what was going on. She recognised how easy it would be to interpret foul play, which would in turn lead to major tension and possibly irreversible damage to an already fragile relationship.

Recognising that her anger and emotion could get in the way of a professional, constructive conversation, she went away to calm down before she approached her colleague. When she felt reasonably calm, she approached him in a private place and simply commented that she noticed there had been a change in the action plan for her client. She forced herself to only ask why the change was needed and then she stopped talking.

Her colleague described a valid reason for the change and she quickly realised that it had been necessary and legitimate. She also realised that had she confronted her colleague in her angry, accusatory state, she would have caused an unnecessary conflict and great discomfort. She would also have made an already difficult relationship even more problematic.

Tackling the Bully

A senior manager noticed that his admin assistant had been distracted and upset for a number of days and asked her what was wrong. Understanding the principles of collaborative leadership, he ensured they had a quiet, private space but he kept the conversation informal to encourage her to talk openly. She confided that the PA of another senior leader had been bullying her for some time. She had been obstructive about providing information, difficult when the admin assistant had needed access to people and resources, and was gossiping and making disparaging comments about her around the office.

The senior manager acknowledged that he felt angry and protective over his colleague, his first inclination was to take over to sort the problem for her. However, he was keen to use his newly learned Coaching for Leadership skills to reflect his confidence in her, support of her, and to assist her to develop the skills to tackle this challenging situation for herself.

He recognised the essential act of attentive listening – it was clear his assistant was having difficulty articulating the problem and was somewhat embarrassed by it. He worked hard to listen without displaying judgment and emotion, despite what he was feeling inside. He wanted her to be able to reflect and explore her own thoughts, uncontaminated by his. He asked simple, open questions to gain the fullest possible information and understanding, without leading the conversation with his own thoughts.

The act of attentive listening alone helped his assistant to calm noticeably and be able to look at the situation more rationally rather than emotionally. Through questions, he then helped her to identify exactly what aspects were causing her the most unhappiness and difficulty. Once they had identified the main issues, he was able to help her to move on to tackle it.

He asked her what she would like to achieve – in other words, what would the situation be like if she could resolve it. Once she had explored this in some detail, his questions progressed to encourage her to consider how she might do this. On occasion, she looked to him for answers and solutions but he avoided giving these. He knew the best outcomes would come from her identifying and working with her own solutions. He helped her to explore different ways of tackling the issue and to identify the pros and cons of each approach. This helped her to identify how she wanted to move forward.

Once she had pinpointed her chosen way forward, he encouraged her to practise what she might say first. When she felt confident, he pinned her down to when she was going to make the approach to the PA. This was important to ensure the assistant didn't pull out and went through with her agreed action. He then agreed a time and date to meet with her again for feedback, review and further support as necessary.

Examples of Managing Accountability and Responsibility

Replacing Difficult with Accountable

The general manager of a large private hospital discussed a member of her night nursing team with whom she had worked for more than 10 years. The nurse worked part time at her facility and part time at a local NHS hospital, always on the night shift. For all this time, the nurse had been branded 'difficult', in that he constantly complained about the practices at the private hospital and compared his work there negatively in comparison to his work at the NHS facility.

Following Coaching for Leadership training, the manager began to realise that an elegant question for him might be: why is he still working at the private facility after all this time if the NHS is so much better? However, her problem and resulting interaction with the nurse was much more about accountability, and she was able to exercise her skills to achieve this when a conflict arose between the day shift and her nurse on the night shift.

It transpired that the day shift had handed over a particular patient-related duty to the nurse, at the change over from the day shift to the night shift. However, the following morning the task had not been completed as it should. This was a serious issue and was reported to the general manager as per procedure. She reflected that prior to her Coaching for Leadership learning, she would have reprimanded the night nurse, and had done so a number of times before. She realised that over the years nothing had changed, so this input was ineffective.

On this occasion, her aim was to use her Coaching for Leadership skills to improve accountability in the practice of her night nurse. She called a meeting between the senior staff on the relevant day and night shift, including her night nurse. She began by laying out her understanding of the problem, simply and without judgment, about behaviours rather than attitudes. She ensured she remained calm and did proportionately less talking and more listening, and she also ensured she employed attentive listening skills.

The night nurse became defensive, and true to form, began to belittle the processes of the facility, stating that if they had the same processes and a particular checklist used by the NHS, then he would have been able to fulfil the task.

The general manager's aim was to hand back the accountability to where it belonged – the night nurse. Her conversation went along these lines:

> Manager: "You feel you could have completed the task if we had a similar checklist to the one you use in the NHS?"
>
> Nurse: "Yes."
>
> Manager: "Do you think it is possible to for us to develop a similar checklist to help with this?"

Nurse: "Yes."

Manager: "Who would be the best person to develop this?"

She reflected that this was a defining question, given it was almost impossible for the nurse not to volunteer himself, given he was the only one who had knowledge of the NHS checklist.

Nurse: "Well I suppose I could have a go at developing it."

Manager: "Great. When do you think you could have a draft ready for us to discuss?"

Again, a defining question to pin down expectations of actions to be taken.

Nurse: "I'll have it for you next Wednesday night, when I'm next on duty."

On the day the work was due, the manager left a message for the nurse, to remind him that she was expecting the draft checklist to be delivered. Just before his shift was due to start, he called in sick. Whilst this was telling, the manager was determined to follow through her intervention, so when the nurse came back on shift the next time, she waited for him. On his arrival, she greeted him and asked for the work he had promised to produce. He looked at her and simply said, "Oh, I didn't think you were serious. We've often talked about work we might do but you've never actually expected us to really do it."

She did follow the process through to its conclusion and the nurse did begin to mellow his disparaging views and get on with his work. However, in her learning reflection, the most profound realisation for her was his comment that he didn't think she was serious. The general manager realised that her lack of follow-through on requests and expectations from her staff had disabled thinking and inhibited responsibility and accountability in her team.

Her staff genuinely thought it didn't matter whether or not they did what they said they would because there was never any follow-up or consequences of not doing it. The manager herself recognised years of frustration, that people around her never did what she asked, encouraged by her own lack of interest and follow-up.

Thereafter, she made a point of meticulously following up on every request and agreement for action. This didn't take much time; most were fast and in passing but it did show her team that she was serious and that she would hold them to account for taking agreed actions. She found her team became more responsive, engaged and accountable for the roles they were paid to do.

Individual or Team

A senior leader had a team member who worked fixed, specific shifts in a 24-hour service. All other team members worked flexible shifts to fit business needs. The team member was particularly inflexible, and this was causing difficulties in covering the service as it changed and took on new business.

Her inflexibility was also causing friction within the team, who were aggrieved that she was allowed to work specific set hours whilst everyone else was required to work flexible shift patterns. Whilst the manager was compassionate regarding people's need to work in ways to accommodate other responsibilities, the situation was causing too much negative impact on the business to ignore.

The manager was fully aware of formal routes to changing employee's work patterns, but every time she attempted this, the team member would take lengthy sick time and initiate further friction amongst her colleagues, with thinly veiled accusations of intimidation. The manager decided to experiment with Coaching for Leadership skills before heading fully into heavyweight employment law procedures.

She realised that she had not shared all the information with her team member, nor had she treated her as an adult, capable of understanding problems and their solutions. She therefore called a meeting and presented the issue factually and without judgment or emotion. She made clear the need for everyone to be working flexibly and was clear that whilst no solution had yet been reached, a solution was nevertheless necessary. This was not negotiable, although the solution itself was.

She then invited the team member to work with her to find a solution to meet the business need. The manager was unsurprised when the team member shrugged, said it was not her problem and that she did not plan to change her working hours. Rather than display her anger, the manager simply asked her team member to take some time to think the problem through and come back to her with her thoughts in a couple of days. She then terminated the meeting to allow her team member to think and reflect.

At the allotted time, her team member did not show for the follow-up meeting. She went to find her, whereupon the team member told her she was resigning. She said she was unable to work any different hours and therefore had decided to seek alternative employment.

Whilst this was not wholly the outcome the general manager had desired, she realised that her team member had reached a solution that was acceptable and relevant to her. They had both avoided lengthy negotiations, conflict and discomfort.

In our learning group, I was able to share that this is not an unusual outcome when using Coaching for Leadership to encourage responsibility and accountability in the workplace. During my original research, many leaders reported that whilst it improved staff retention rates in the long term, initially leaders lost members of their team. When I investigated this, it seems that leaders weren't unhappy with this. Those that were leaving were those who had avoided accountability the most. They were staff members who gave little to the service and lacked motivation for themselves and their role. Leaders said that it was as if they facilitated people to go who needed to go, and it was in a kind way, which avoided lengthy and distressing formal performance management procedures. You could say it was with love.

Accountability with Compassion

A nursing home manager described a problem she had encountered with a member of her care staff on the night shift. She had come to the care home in the early hours of the morning to undertake an unannounced audit visit as required by the regulator. The night team were unaware the visit was to take place, as per protocol.

At around 5am, the manager looked for her team around the building and noticed that one of the rostered staff was missing. When she asked her team-mates where she was, she noticed that they became uncomfortable; they either said they didn't know where she was or made a vague suggestion of her whereabouts. It became clear that the team were covering for their absent colleague. When the manager went to locate clocking on/off data, she realised that this carer had been leaving the premises two hours before the end of her shift, on the same day each week, for the past two months.

The manager was very aware of the seriousness of the situation. Certain numbers and combinations of staff are a legal requirement in the sector. If there had been a formal audit by the regulator, this would have had extremely serious consequences, and as it was, the situation would have to be formally reported. The manager was furious that her trust had been breached, that the team were covering it up and, by her own admission, her inclination was to bring the full force of disciplinary action down on her team member.

She was, however, keen to experiment with her new Coaching for Leadership learning in the first instance. She called the carer in for a meeting. Due to the seriousness of the issue, it needed to be formal. Nevertheless, she was determined to remain calm and maintain a collaborative leadership style. She began by laying out her observation – of what she had discovered and why it was so serious. Whilst the carer was a young woman, the manager was careful to treat her as a fellow adult and spoke honestly but without emotion and judgment. She then simply asked why the carer had been leaving early.

The carer broke down in tears, explaining that she had a terminally ill mother who she was caring for at home. While she was at work, a personal carer was employed to look after her mother, but she had been unable to cover two hours per week – those hours when she was leaving work early. She needed to go home so that her mother was not alone.

The manager reflected to her learning group what an impossible situation she felt it to be. A very serious breach had occurred, but she felt it was imperative to deal with it well; her team member was well regarded, a good worker and she didn't want to lose her from the team. As a care manager, her instinct was to step in and sort the situation herself. However, she knew that collaborative leadership demanded that she facilitate her team member to find the solution for herself.

The manager was careful to lay out the situation clearly and to make clear that it could not continue. She then asked her team member to go away and think about how things might be rectified. She was careful to remain supportive without being parental and refraining from offering her own thoughts and advice. It was important to her that she reflected she cared for her staff as much as they did for their residents.

Later, the team member returned and announced that she had sorted the problem. She had discussed her problem with trusted colleagues. One of her colleagues on the day shift had offered to come in two hours early on the problem shift day to cover her so that she could go home to take care of her mother. It was a simple and effective solution.

The manager reflected that whilst there were the issues of staff covering unauthorised absence and lack of responsibility, she felt most sad that a competent adult had opted for a dangerous solution rather than thinking through a responsible resolution. She realised that her staff weren't functioning with adult, switched-on thinking; they opted for childlike ignorance over professional thinking and problem solving. She resolved to continue to develop her own collaborative leadership skills to ensure she could continue to function compassionately, whilst expecting the best from her team.

Examples of Benefits Outside the Workplace

A final couple of anecdotes highlight that coaching skills can work outside of the workplace as well as in it. Many leaders have reflected that it works with husbands, families, children and teenagers too.

Getting the Hallway Painted

One leader commented that she had been trying to get her husband to decorate their hallway for around six months. Despite all the months of nagging, cajoling and getting upset, the hallway remained unpainted. After her Coaching for Leadership learning she went home and simply said to her husband, "Even though we've been talking about it for ages, the hallway still isn't decorated. What shall we do so we can get it done soon?" She then left the subject and carried on with her evening as normal.

To her surprise she came home the next day and the hallway was painted. On reflecting why this might have happened, she concluded that her former requests for her husband to do it had been full of emotion and criticism. She had been telling him to do it and how rather than leaving him to deal with it in his own way. She realised her behaviour had switched him off from taking responsibility and that by giving feedback and asking a question, he found a way to motivate himself and get the job done.

Teenagers and Their Bedrooms

A senior leader confided that he had been having months of arguments and conflicts with his teenage son over the mess in his bedroom. The problem was so bad that the smell from the room was pervading the house and the manager was embarrassed to have visitors to his home. There had been hours of screaming, shouting, demands and reprimands, but nothing worked and the bedroom was still as bad as ever.

The leader decided to Give the Feedback, Ask the Question as an experiment. He simply made a comment about the state of the room and why it was affecting the rest of the house. He ensured he was calm before he said it and he made no criticism or sarcastic comment as he might have done before. He then asked his son how he was going to rectify it, then turned and walked away.

By his own admission, his son's room can't yet be considered tidy. It is however slightly improved, and dialogue has opened between him and his son about it. They are able to talk about it without shouting and arguing and he feels his son is starting to realise the impact of his messy room on the rest of the household. It isn't a problem which will be wholly sorted in the short term, but the leader felt he had at least been able to move things forward by behaving with love.

Looking at these examples on face value, it might not be easy to see how love is of any relevance to leading others, or to using Coaching for Leadership to get the best from yourself, your service and your people. And yet if you look closely it's there in every corner. You don't have to say it out loud and you don't have to be overt about it, but unless you acknowledge that you care, you'll always have a team who are only part-functional.

Traditional directive forms of leadership are what we're accustomed to. We're raised to think that managers manage – they are the boss who has to be seen to know what to do, take control and help their employees by giving instructions, opinions and orders. These types of leadership are reinforced by TV and media, where blame, excuses, aggressive competition and being 'top dog' are encouraged.

But sadly, these practices don't create great teams and they don't assure good business. This only comes from leading in a way that brings humanity back into the workplace. When we understand how human beings and human brains work best, to their full capacity, that's when we create cultures and environments that deliver the most profitable outcomes.

When people are engaged, accountable and adult in the workplace, it matters to the bottom line. Quality, customer service, output and productivity are all dependent on people working to their best. Best doesn't happen when brains are switched off and people feel they are treated like children or commodities.

To get the best out of people you have to love. It's not soppy or unbusinesslike, it's just common sense. People function at their best when treated with respect, compassion, value and care. These are all core components of the philosophical concept of love.

So, I would urge you to Love to Lead. Practise the techniques, exercise the principles, do the experiments and watch your people and business flourish in the love.

About the Author

Tracy has many years of experience in the design, delivery, implementation and evaluation of learning and leadership development programmes. Her work is focused on achieving strategic and operational leadership excellence and a defined return on investment for organisations.

She has coined the term 'Give the Feedback, Ask the Question' to describe the caring techniques of working with teams and individuals, to ensure maximum functioning and engagement from all whose performance is fundamental to business success and growth. Tracy has extensive experience in executive and leadership coaching, specialising in psychological approaches to ensure long-term, sustainable behavioural and cognitive development.

Tracy has spent most of her career in health and care environments. She has a Master's degree in Management of Change from the University of Sussex and is a Doctor of Philosophy. She made an original contribution to the body of knowledge in leadership and leadership coaching practice by combining the ethics and philosophies of 'caring' with the need for leaders to be able to deliver sound return on investment and business success. She has developed a model of coaching which incorporates an ethos of 'Care' to signpost leaders to appreciate the importance of equality of focus on people, organisational culture and business processes, in fully realising business potential.

As founding director of Kite Consulting for Leadership and Management, Tracy personally works with individuals and organisations to ensure excellence in learning, leadership and organisational development. She is Director of Learning and Leadership Development at The Regard Group.

Website: www.leadershipaspirations.co.uk

Email: kiteconsulting@sky.com

Notes:

Notes:

Notes:

Notes:

Notes:

Printed by Amazon Italia Logistica S.r.l.
Torrazza Piemonte (TO), Italy

10460603R00134